Struggle and Suffrage in Morpeth and Northumberland

Struggle and Suffrage in Morpeth and Northumberland

Craig Armstrong

PEN & SWORD
HISTORY

AN IMPRINT OF PEN & SWORD BOOKS LTD
YORKSHIRE - PHILADELPHIA

First published in Great Britain in 2020 by
Pen & Sword History
An imprint of
Pen & Sword Books Limited
Yorkshire - Philadelphia

ISBN 978 1 52671 9 652

A CIP catalogue record for this book is available from the British Library

Printed and bound in the UK
by 4edge Ltd, Essex, SS5 4AD

Pen & Sword Books Limited incorporates the imprints of Atlas,
Archaeology, Aviation, Discovery, Family History, Fiction, History, Maritime,
Military, Military Classics, Politics, Select, Transport, True Crime, Air World,
Frontline Publishing, Leo Cooper, Remember When, Seaforth Publishing,
The Praetorian Press, Wharncliffe Local History, Wharncliffe Transport,
Wharncliffe True Crime and White Owl.

For a complete list of Pen & Sword titles please contact
PEN & SWORD BOOKS LIMITED
47 Church Street, Barnsley, South Yorkshire S70 2AS, United Kingdom
E-mail: enquiries@pen-and-sword.co.uk
Website: www.pen-and-sword.co.uk
Or
PEN AND SWORD BOOKS
1950 Lawrence Rd, Havertown, PA 19083, USA
E-mail: Uspen-and-sword@casematepublishers.com
Website: www.penandswordbooks.com

Contents

Introduction

Northumberland was, and remains, a sparsely populated county and, according to the 2001 census, had the lowest population density in England with just sixty-two people per square kilometre. The total population in 2001 was just 307,190. These factors impacted on the development of the county and the population throughout the nineteenth and early twentieth centuries dwelled largely in small – by British standards – market and former market towns and in widely scattered small villages and hamlets.

For the women of the county, life could at times be harsh and a degree of resilience and self-reliance was often a necessity. Although traditionally a patriarchal society, women, especially older women, had significant and often unseen influence upon their menfolk. Lying on the Scottish border as it does, Northumberland and its inhabitants had been strongly influenced by border history and many observers stated that the Northumbrian character was more in keeping with the Scottish borderer than their English neighbours. This, to a large extent, remains true, and the historical and cultural links remain strong between the two areas. Some even claimed that this had an influence upon attitudes towards marriage and sexual behaviour among both men and women.

The largely rural county was dependent upon agriculture, and a unique system that relied upon female labour developed and continued throughout the period. Other than agriculture, the county developed an economically powerful and influential coalfield in the south-east, while fishing played a significant role in the coastal economy. Until 1400 Newcastle had been a part of the county, but this city had then been designated as a county in its own right, although it still exerted a strong economic and social influence over Northumberland. It was only in 1844 that the historic shires of Bedlingtonshire, Islandshire and Norhamshire were incorporated into the county, having previously been under the power of the bishops of Durham.

This book considers in a very broad sense the lives of the women of Northumberland. An in-depth study of every aspect of women's lives in the county is impossible given the brevity of the current book, but it is hoped that a very good idea of the challenges that faced the women of Northumberland can be discerned from these pages.

Particular consideration is given to the impact of the suffragist movement and, especially, to the life and untimely death of Miss Emily Wilding Davison. The radical suffragette has become one of the heroines of Northumberland, spoken of in the same awed tones as those reserved for women such as Grace Darling. Miss Davison's memory has become a rallying cry for feminism in the region (and beyond), but the truth is that she was not born in the county (although she had extremely strong family links to Northumberland and loved the county throughout her brief life) and spent relatively little time here. Nevertheless, Emily, a complex character whose life remains, in some respects, shrouded in mystery, has become synonymous with Northumberland and its women's spirit of determination and independence.

The book also includes two chapters giving a very brief overview of the impact that the two world wars had upon the women of Northumberland and the significant part they played in maintaining morale, supporting the armed forces, protecting the home front and working as part of the war effort.

CHAPTER ONE

Victorian Northumberland

For those women who were born into and lived in rural Northumberland opportunities and options were far more limited than for their counterparts who resided in the larger towns. Agriculture in Northumberland was unique in England during the Victorian period in the number of women who were employed in labour and by the employment terms that governed their lives. In the rural parts of the county, the system known as bondage held sway for many years.

The women hired on as bondagers at the annual hirings, which were a feature of the Northumbrian market towns. At these hiring fairs agreements would be made between the farmers and male labourers (known locally as hinds) whereby payment, both in cash and in kind, would be agreed along with accommodation and, for much of the century, a common contractual stipulation that the labourer would also provide a bondager for a term of either six or twelve months. The bondager, unlike the hind, was guaranteed pay only for the days she worked and wages varied depending upon the type of labour that was carried out on a particular day. The bondagers could be clearly identified as they wore a form of unofficial uniform consisting of a distinctive bonnet (quite often referred to as an 'ugly'), headscarf, blouse (often blue), sackings around the legs and striped woollen skirts, below which were, if they were lucky, hard-wearing boots.

There were two other options within the field of agriculture for Northumbrian women. In the south of Northumberland, particularly around Newcastle and Morpeth, women frequently hired themselves on as casual labour on a daily basis. This was especially common during important periods such as the harvest, but was, obviously, dependent upon the closeness of town and farm, along with the fact that such a woman required another source of income.

The other category of female labourer was the cottar. This was a field that was open only to single women or widows and such women were hired directly by the farmer for a specified contract period. The contract most often included a rent-free cottage and some basic provision of coal and potatoes throughout the term of the contract (usually twelve months). In return for this provision the cottar agreed to be available to work on the farm when required for an agreed daily wage. In some cases a mother and daughter were taken on and this was referred to as a double cottar. For the cottar such an agreement provided a degree of security in terms of both employment and living conditions, but the use of cottars was growing increasingly uncommon as the system had several weaknesses. It depended upon a farmer having sufficient empty cottages on his property to employ cottars and there was some moral disquiet over women working in such conditions where they were removed from a patriarchal family structure. For the farmer, it was often more economical to fill a vacant cottage with a hind and his family or a hind and hired bondager.

The conditions faced by female agricultural labourers varied widely, depending on factors such as the attitude of their employer and the traditions of the area. The dukes of Northumberland, for example, were keen throughout the nineteenth century to be seen as improving the lot of their farm labourers and to limit and even eliminate the dependence upon bondagers on their lands. They were, however, a rare example and, despite a steady decline in female labour as the century went on, female agricultural workers still made up 25 per cent of the farm labourers in Northumberland and 12.5 per cent of the total for the entirety of England during the 1890s. So vital was the contribution of the female farm labourer to the agricultural economy of Northumberland that in 1867 the Hexham Board of Guardians stated that the prohibition of female labour would simply lead to a prohibition on farming in the county.

The peculiar system of relying upon female agricultural labour in Northumberland arose from several factors, but one of the most important was the sheer scarcity of labour in the sparsely populated county. Rural Northumberland in the nineteenth century was very sparsely populated indeed, and villages were few and widely scattered. Even the villages themselves would often have been classed as nothing more than hamlets by those used to the larger populations of the south. A great many of the population lived on isolated farms in cottages that varied immensely in terms of living conditions. Employment choice for women was further limited by the scarcity of industries such as textile manufacture and, for many women from the area, the higher wages on offer for farm labourers was a continuing attraction and draw.

The isolated communities of Glendale in north Northumberland typify this. In the census returns throughout the century for Glendale it can clearly be seen that women far exceeded the numbers of men. The population of the area declined throughout the century, but it is clear that men were leaving in greater numbers and at a greater rate than were women.

Glendale, with its dependence on sheep farming, was an area that remained popular with bondagers and in 1851 the census reveals that 24 per cent of women were involved in agricultural work and 15 per cent were noted as being full-time agricultural labourers. This compares with similar average figures of 8.5 per cent and 3 per cent respectively for the rest of Northumberland. Twenty years later, the number had decreased to 16 per cent, but this was partially explained by the fact that the category of farmer's wife had been eliminated from the total, despite the fact that the vast majority of farmer's wives could certainly be said to be working on the land.

This difference in the ratio between men and women had other effects upon women's lives in the rural hinterlands. Women living in such areas were far less likely to get married, and when they did so, they were often older. The census of 1871 reveals that in Glendale an astounding 52 per cent of women aged 20 to

45 were unmarried compared to an average of just 34 per cent in the rest of England and Wales. This was not solely down to a scarcity of men. The census returns also show that fewer men got married in the area and this is perhaps explained, at least partially, by the transitory nature of the hiring system which saw people moving from area to area on a yearly and sometimes even more frequent basis.

Bondagers were hired almost solely on the basis of their perceived physical strength and hardiness. The hiring fairs must often have been akin to slave auctions, with farmers and hinds assessing women who wished to be employed, in a purely physical and distant manner. The job status of the women was clearly shown by those who remained unhired wearing tickets, these being replaced with red ribbons upon agreement of a contract.

A study of the bondagers of Glendale shows that many lived in with established families consisting of a hind, his wife and children. These bondagers were most often between the ages of 15 and 24 and a substantial number of them came from Scotland (with smaller numbers from Ireland). Even those from Northumberland were often found far from the place where they had been born and kinship links for such young women appear to have frequently been broken by the bondage system.

The impact of some of the developments of the agricultural revolution had led to an increase in the number of farm jobs that were seen as being particularly suited to the employment of women. Turnip production for the fattening of the sheep upon which so much of Northumbrian farming depended, for example, required a year-long cycle of cultivation, and the bondager was seen as ideal for this work.

The tasks facing the bondager were varied and typically involved very heavy exertion. Typically, a bondager could expect to work for a minimum of twelve hours per day throughout the summer, with longer periods during the harvest and in winter from sunrise to sunset. As well as taking part in active work in the fields, bondagers, and for that matter cottars, would be expected to help with tasks such as maintaining byres and cleaning such facilities.

Typical Yearly Tasks of the Bondager

Month	Tasks
January	Pulling turnips, working in barns
February	"
March	Stoning
April	Stoning, turnip-hoeing and backing
May	"
June	Quickening and hay-harvesting
July	"
August	Turnip-hoeing, corn harvest
September	Corn harvest, gathering potatoes
October	"
November	Gathering potatoes
December	Pulling turnips

The system caused some disruption to typical family life as the heavy labour required could not always be performed at various stages in a woman's life. Pregnancy and the rearing of very young children often precluded a hind's wife from taking part in her bondaging role and required the hind to hire on another woman at additional cost to the family. As a woman grew older it was also likely that she might not be able to make a full contribution, so many hinds with older wives were often forced to hire on a woman specifically as a bondager. An apprentice at the farm of Lilburn Grange observed in 1842 that a hind with an older wife was far worse off than one with a younger wife or a young bondager hired specifically.[1]

Attitudes towards the female agricultural labourers of Northumberland were ambivalent. In the rural parts of the county itself they were simply looked on as an established part of the community, but for others they were a dangerous threat to established society and their way of life was a threat to their own moral rectitude. Some viewed the heavy work routine of the bondager as fostering a healthy superior woman. Numerous accounts celebrated the bondager as being superior in strength, skill and education to their counterparts in the south of England, while others celebrated the fact that the bondager could cope with work every bit as arduous as that of their male counterparts.

To others, the muscular form of womanhood embodied by the bondager was a gross threat. The fact that bondagers were often simply referred to as 'the body' meant that attitudes towards them could not be separated from the physical. The bondagers themselves were more than aware of these links. The concentration on their physicality at the hiring fairs was more than enough proof of this and for those who were of small stature or advancing in years the experience could no doubt be humiliating, but for others their brawn was a source of pride and the fact that the bondagers wore a form of uniform which was neither provided nor compulsory was seen as a source of that pride.

Some critics of the approach pointed out that bondagers hired solely on account of their strength could be of bad character and that their presence among workers who were otherwise of good character could lead to a pollution of morals. This attitude, which seemed to automatically assume that bondagers were of lesser moral character, was encouraged among some by the celebratory excess that marked the conclusion of hiring fairs. Typically, in the afternoon of the fair there was dancing and drinking and this, critics claimed, inevitably led to a decline in morally acceptable behaviour and even debauchery. The local clergy were particularly vociferous in their criticism and claimed that the illicit sexual behaviour and the drunkenness that attended hiring fairs was a consequence of the lack of organized recreational pursuits.

There was also, especially away from the areas in which they were commonplace, some approbation attached to the term bondager, which had come to represent a young unmarried woman who worked in shared accommodation with a farmhand in an isolated area of the county. Following on from the criticism voiced in the paragraph above regarding the activities at the hiring fairs, there were also criticisms over the living conditions of the bondagers. Unmarried bondagers, often fit and active young women, were housed in the same cottages as the hind who had hired them. Often these cottages had only one room and thus man and woman were forced to dress and undress in the company of each other. In such surroundings the 'uncontrolled sexuality of the bondager could work its particular disordering mischief',[2] causing hinds, married or unmarried, to become distracted and unsettled by these 'coarse blowzy girls'.[3]

The moral reformers insisted that bondagers and other female labourers should be provided with their own rooms to limit the licentious behaviour encouraged by shared accommodation. Such work, however, was halting and could only be undertaken with the co-operation of the farmers or landowners and many of these were not overly concerned with the moral rectitude of the women they employed when compared with the wholesale alterations that would have been required to their properties and the attendant costs.

For many of those opposed to the system of using female workers as found in Northumberland, the fear was exacerbated by the belief that prolonged exposure to manual work in the farm environment led inevitably to moral degradation. While some cited living conditions, others, perhaps more worldly, placed the blame on exposure to the morally poor conversations that could take place in the working environment of the bondager. Armed with such beliefs, these moralists claimed, against most evidence, that female farm workers were more predisposed to immoral behaviour than, for example, those in domestic service.

Still others feared for the femininity of the bondagers and cottars, claiming that the very nature of their hard physical work rendered them less feminine and imposed upon them a sort of masculinity which rendered them unattractive and therefore less likely to marry and, in wedlock, to bear children and then act as capable mothers. Several of these commentators claimed that although the bondagers possessed great skill in farming tasks, this was to the detriment of skills traditionally associated with femininity and motherhood. This criticism of the housekeeping skills of Northumbrian women in the nineteenth century was a common one, but the bondager was particularly criticized. One writer claimed that an aged Northumbrian shepherd who had been interviewed claimed that he had remained unmarried because a 'woman in Northumberland's not worth house room'.[4]

Even those female workers who had properties to themselves were not exempt from suspicion and implied criticism. Many of the moral reformers saw the practice of housing single women on their own in vacant cottages as even more dangerous than housing them with a hind and it was stated that this was a 'great cause of immorality'.[5] Once more the woman was made out as both the cause and the victim of moral degeneration and there was no such criticism of male workers being housed on their own, despite evidence that in many cases such hinds often had women in their homes for celebrations and such.

The moralists pointed to the fact that rates of illegitimacy were considerably higher in rural Northumberland than they were in the more urban areas. The reasons for this remain obscure, but it would seem that bondagers made up a relatively small percentage of this group when compared to women who worked as domestic servants or who still lived at home. Once more, however, this cannot be proven or taken as fact as the evidence is extremely fragmentary.

It seemed that the birth of an illegitimate child was not seen as being a particular drawback or shameful by many of those who lived in rural Northumberland at the time. Archdeacon Hamilton, for example, decried the fact that those who lived in north Northumberland had a particularly lax attitude towards sexuality and to the institution of marriage, perhaps influenced by long tradition on the Border Marches. Hamilton, a moral reformer if there ever was one, was particularly appalled by the willingness of the rural community of Northumberland to overlook any stigma attached by wider society to illegitimate motherhood or birth. Despite the concerns of the good archdeacon, the tolerant attitude among isolated farming communities continued well into the twentieth century, with examples being given of a female farm worker being taken off the fields for a brief period and the farmer simply being told the reason was that she had that morning 'had a wean in the barn'.[6] The unfortunate young woman returned to work shortly afterwards.

The presence of an illegitimate child certainly did not seem to hinder the employment of women as cottars and other agricultural labourers. This tolerant attitude was not replicated outside the immediate farming communities, however, and many urged that women who had fallen morally, in their opinion, and conceived and birthed illegitimate children should be harshly punished through punitive measures which would make it increasingly difficult for them to find employment. The end of such a strategy would inevitably have ended up with the mother in the workhouse.

Landowners seem to have been more concerned with demonstrating that, although bastardy was rife, the morals of their female workers were otherwise healthy. Comparisons between rural and urban women were again used in this respect. One landowner, testifying to the 1867 commission, stated that despite high rates of illegitimacy, there was no prostitution as there was in the more urban areas. This debate over the bad influence of the town over innocent female farm labourers continued throughout the century. At the end of the Victorian era, Northumbrian clergymen claimed that during the hirings the streetwise cuteness of the urban dweller had the opportunity to mingle with the innocence of the rural woman and that this often led to licentious behaviour and a decline in moral rectitude.

To many of the critics, the bondager represented a grave threat to the stability of rural society in Northumberland. The presence of so many young females who were also highly mobile within their limited society was a threat not only to themselves but also to the men with whom they worked. The perceived lack of control exerted over the bondagers and other female workers was also seen as being harmful to their characters.

Such concerns as those mentioned above were not so different from those being expressed in more urban settings such as Newcastle or the larger urban centres of Northumberland such as Hexham, Morpeth or Alnwick. The main difference for the reformers in the rural setting was that there were not the facilities for supervising and educating women as the female farm workers were far more mobile and isolated.

The clergy and other moralists were also vociferous about the system of annually changing employer in mid-May, a process known as flitting. This annual movement was seen as causing unnecessary upheaval and resulted in a lessening of the influence of the employers as well as other possible forces for good such as schoolmasters and, of course, the clergy. Philanthropy was also curtailed by the flitting as the transience of the farm workers meant that improvements could not be focused and therefore lost impetus. Farmers and landowners alike recognized the problem of a highly mobile workforce. As the century progressed, the landowners in Northumberland made efforts to discourage the mass movement of their workers. Some offered rewards to faithful workers. Jane Long gives the example of an Anne Armytage being awarded £3 as a reward for giving three years' service at a Kirkwhelpington farm as early as 1843.[7]

Over the course of the nineteenth century there were three parliamentary reports detailing the status of the female farm worker. These were published in 1843, 1867 and 1893 respectively. The first two concentrated solely on the conditions of women and children in agriculture, while the third, and most comprehensive, was more broadly focused on the agricultural labourer in general. The first report, at least the Northumberland section, can be largely dismissed as its author Sir Francis Doyle simply asked farmers and landowners their opinions and did not trouble himself to interview any of the workers themselves. What emerged, unsurprisingly, was a positive report which claimed that the women and children were happy, enjoyed good conditions and were well educated and healthy. The only dissenting voice came from the town clerk of Morpeth, who raised concerns over the effect that working in the fields had upon the moral rectitude and standards of young women.

The second report was more thorough. Conducted by J.J. Henley, an Oxfordshire landowner, magistrate and Poor Law guardian, the report was more critical but, once again, the number of actual workers interviewed and the importance placed upon their evidence was overwhelmed by that given to the testimony of landowners and, particularly, to the large number (approximately sixty) of professionals – mainly clergymen, doctors and teachers – which Mr Henley relied upon. By depending upon the testimony of these professionals, who were overwhelmingly reformists, Henley's report was skewed towards a view that reform was needed and the report focused far more on the tensions that developed over the mixing of sexes in agricultural labour.

The attitudes expressed by some of these professionals, however, occasionally varied. While the clergymen and teachers were overwhelmingly in favour of reforms and the vast majority were critical of the use of female labour, the doctors expressed more mixed opinions. Some doctors claimed that the labour in the fields produced women who were good bearers of children and another, Dr F. Cahill, stated that 'female complaints' were less common in those who worked in the fields. Others, however, said that the strains of field work were particularly arduous for married women and those who had children, and could result in a decline in health. Such testimony, given in the 1867 report, resulted in the author firmly asserting that labour in the fields resulted in healthy young women who went on to make fine wives for labourers and who made good mothers in their social class.

Some of the positive testimony given by doctors was no doubt influenced by a comparison between women in the rural setting with their urban counterparts. One Berwick surgeon, called to give his opinion, stated that in his view farm women were far more healthy and that such moral decline that could be seen in the countryside was largely brought about by town women travelling into the rural areas as casual labour during the harvest and bringing their bad morals and slovenly habits with them.

As the nineteenth century went on and technology was gradually introduced and developed, the traditional division of labour along gender lines became even more pronounced. Scything, for example, was seen as exclusively a male job, while the use of the sickle was not only available to women but many experts asserted that women were more efficient with this instrument than men. On many Northumbrian farms this resulted in female workers with sickles being relegated to a role in which they helped to tidy up the mess that had been made by the faster but messier scythes wielded by the men. Likewise, ploughing and carting were the preserve of men, with Henley claiming in his report that witnesses had testified that carting was a dangerous task for which women lacked the necessary skills. This was a divisive subject, with many of the female workers claiming that they not only had the skills necessary for the task but that they enjoyed it.

The jobs to which women were allocated mirrored many of those found elsewhere among those who did not work as agricultural labourers, in that they tended to be dirty and monotonous tasks. In some cases the demarcation matched that found in other industries. The loading of manure, for example, was seen as an exclusively female task and many farmers reported that hinds would refuse to undertake the job and would instead stand idle while the bondagers got on with the task.

One of the key reasons for this demarcation of tasks was that the interests of the male workers were best served by ensuring that the skilled tasks remained firmly in their preserve. The 1893 report grasped this fact, stating that the women were almost as effective as the men at most tasks but at a significantly reduced cost and that female labour would remain, as employers could not afford to replace female workers with hinds due to the increased cost of wages.

The attitude of hinds towards the bondage system was complex. There is some evidence that many hinds resented the system and the presence of the bondagers, and unsuccessful attempts were made in the 1830s, 1860s and 1870s to overturn the bondage system as a condition of employment. The hinds simply did not have enough power to enforce their demands in the face of determined opposition from the farmers and many of the landowners. In 1861, for example, attempts were made by hinds at both Alnwick and Belford to resist the condition of employing a bondager. The attempts ended in failure, with such hinds being left unemployed by the farmers who were present at the hirings.

The female workers, conversely, had far more power as their services were so much in demand. Just twelve years after the failed attempts of the hinds mentioned earlier, female farm workers at the hiring fair at Haydon Bridge mounted a successful strike, which resulted in them receiving higher wages. This, of course, further stirred resentment in many hinds with some having contracts cancelled after they were subsequently unable to negotiate suitable conditions of employment with a bondager.

The situation faced by married hinds who had to bring with them a bondager was an intriguing one, which often found the unfortunate young female bondager heavily criticized. There were repeated allegations that bondagers were useless in the home and that they caused trouble in the families of hinds. Many hinds' wives objected to the lack of privacy which their situation afforded and were concerned over the possible temptations that such close living placed in the path of their husbands. One Northumbrian wife of a hind told the 1867 report that their young hind had to undress in the same room as her husband and claimed that this was un-Christian, perhaps hiding deeper fears.

Despite all these fears, however, the position of the female farm labourer was never under serious threat in Northumberland during the nineteenth century. The rural economy simply depended upon the women far too much for the system to be dismantled. At Wooler, at the heartland of the bondager system, a local bank manager stated that public opinion would be firmly against any such move, while a farmer at Ilderton stated to the 1867 report that his overseer had orders to prevent levity in the conversations which took place between the sexes while working in the fields and that a farmer who enforced strict supervision over his female workers could ensure that the morals of the female workers could be upheld (note, the morals of the male workers were not in doubt).

Opportunities in the more urban areas of Northumberland were more varied for women, but this was often a smokescreen hiding a multitude of problems and a lack of opportunity for women to find stimulating and well-paid work. For many, the drudgery of bringing up an often large family in dwellings that often were little better than slums, on insufficient income and with poor food and sanitization was the norm.

Morpeth, as one of the main towns in Northumberland, had found fame as a cattle market and was for some time the largest cattle market in the north of England. The subsequent growth of the town saw its population expand rapidly. The population of the township of Morpeth in 1801 stood at just 2,951, while by 1881 this had risen to 5,068. The majority of this expansion had taken place in the working-class areas of the town. Housing stocks and sanitary facilities did not keep pace with this development. The authorities attempted to improve matters by laying down a number of bye-laws which ordered the townspeople, particularly those living in the less salubrious parts of the town, to contribute to the cleaning of the town. Those living in the tenements of the Back Riggs, for example, had a responsibility to clean the channels, drains, gutters and sewers that ran adjacent to their properties. If they failed to do so, they could be fined the not inconsiderable sum of £5.

The Yards and Riggs of Morpeth hosted tenement buildings alongside coach-houses, privies, stables, sheds, wash-houses and workshops, and the resultant atmosphere in these areas was one of filth and poverty. A government inspector, however, did find some cause to praise the housewives of these areas, stating that where possible the women kept their properties as clean as they could and that it was a common practice, having washed the stone floor, to sprinkle it with white sand.

In 1851, some 516 Morpeth women had jobs that necessitated working outside their own homes. The vast majority of these jobs were poorly paid, with 293 of them being forms of domestic service or washer-women. A further 130 were employed in trades involving the making and retailing of food and/or drink, while 51 were employed in making clothes or shoes, 31 were employed in agriculture (largely as labourers), and the remaining 11 had found somewhat better-paid roles as teachers or instructors.

A report in 1849 was damning of the conditions found within the town, stating that typhus was prevalent along with scarlet fever, tuberculosis and whooping cough. These illnesses caused a high death rate among infants and there was a very high prevalence of illegitimate births among the poorer population in Morpeth. A few years previously there had been an outbreak of cholera in which a woman died in the filthy and overcrowded Lumsden Lane. Meanwhile, in Union Street, the inspector found that the properties had no yards on the east side and that this resulted in waste being thrown into the street, while the liquid refuse which emanated from privies and cesspits was left to stand for too long and these facilities were not emptied regularly enough.

At the time of the inspector's visit, Morpeth had thirty lodging houses and these, too, were in a sorry state. Several did not even have beds, while others were crammed with beds packed tightly together with some residents finding room beneath beds and on the limited floor space. Sanitary arrangements consisted of 'a tub filled with vomit and natural evacuations'.[8] These rough boarding houses made no discrimination between gender or age, with men, women and children packed closely together. Conditions in the local workhouse also came in for criticism, with the inspector claiming that, as a result of the poor housing in the town, its infirmary was packed with typhus cases.

Some women in the towns of Northumberland could make their way in the running of their own business but, once again, opportunities were limited. A trade directory of 1887 shows us that in Morpeth (for which the vast majority of entries are male) there were women employed in the running of a variety of widely differing professions, trades and industries as follows:

Female Entries in Morpeth Directory of 1887

Directory Entry	Number
Academies and Schools	9
Beerhouses	1
Berlin Wool & Fancy Repositories	2
Booksellers, Stationers & Newsagents	1
Boot & Shoe Makers	5
Butchers	2
China, Glass & Earthenware Dealers	2
Coal Merchants	1
Confectioners	3
Cowkeepers	4
Farmers	1
Fruiterers & Grocers	4
General Dealers	1
Grocers, Tea Dealers, etc.	5
Hairdressers	1
Hosiers & Haberdashers	5
Hotels, Inns & Taverns	5
Joiners & Builders	1
Linen & Woollen Drapers	2
Livery Stables & Proprietors	2
Lodgings & Apartments	10
Milliners & Dressmakers	16
Printers, Letterpress	1
Plumbers & Gas Fitters	1
Refreshment Rooms	2
Registry Office for Servants	2
Shopkeepers	3
Tripe Dressers (black/white pudding-makers)	1
Watchmakers & Jewellers	2

At first glance this is a wide variety of careers but in some cases the same woman is undertaking several different roles, while the majority of jobs are those which traditionally were open to women such as managing lodging houses (ten of the thirteen lodging houses are listed under the names of women) or as milliners or dressmakers. There are certainly some surprises which indicate either women breaking through traditional gender demarcations or are evidence of a widow or daughter taking over a business previously run by a man. Examples of these include Isabelle Daglish who is listed under plumbers and gasfitters at 23 Bridge Street, and Mary Manners who is listed as a builder and joiner at 19 Oldgate Street.

Away from the fields, the women of Northumberland were proving that they were more than willing to embrace and to fight for changes in their circumstances. We have already heard of striking bondagers, but the nascent campaign for women's suffrage also gained early footholds in the county.

While Newcastle was always the epicentre of suffragist organization in the north-east, the smaller communities of Northumberland also played a substantial role. Morpeth, for example, had been an early starter in the campaign for women's suffrage. On 30 April 1869, the town presented a petition in favour of women's suffrage. In March 1872, a large meeting was held in North Shields where huge numbers of tradespeople, workers and seafarers attended to hear speeches from several people including the famed working-class suffragist Jessie Hannah Craigen (c.1835–99). Throughout the 1870s, famous suffrage campaigners including Jessie Craigen, Alice Scatcherd and Lydia Becker all gave speeches at Morpeth.[9]

On 11 December 1893, a large meeting was held at St Oswin's Hall in Tynemouth where Mrs Millicent Fawcett and a number of other speakers talked on the subject of extending women's suffrage. The well-known local suffragist Mrs Mona Taylor presided and opened the meeting by telling the crowd that progress had been made as those women, from all political persuasions, who campaigned for women's suffrage were no longer talked of as being 'wild women' and had gained a measure of respectability for the cause. Mrs Taylor went on to congratulate the women of Hexham and Newcastle for raising support from across all political beliefs and from all sections of society, before expressing the hope that this would also prove the case in Tynemouth.

Mrs Fawcett told the audience, rather optimistically, that the government had accepted the view of the House of Commons that the franchise be conferred upon rate-paying women with respect to the parish councils. She also highlighted the progress being made by women in other parts of the world, telling the assembly that the women of New Zealand had just participated in their first election. In sharp contrast to the cross-society emphasis given by Mrs Taylor, Mrs Fawcett told the audience that it was absurd to deny women the vote as many were already 'landowners, householders, heads of large businesses, [and] considerable employers of labour'. Perhaps aware of how this sounded, she added that the cause should apply to all women, regardless of wealth. Mrs Fawcett then told the audience that it should be pointed out that women's suffrage did not mean female MPs but the right for women who were 'house-holding or rate-paying' members of society to vote for MPs.[10]

In response to criticisms that giving women the vote could lead to political upheaval, Mrs Fawcett cited the example of the Isle of Man where women had possessed the vote for thirteen years and had proven themselves trustworthy even to those who had been opposed to giving them suffrage, including two former governors of the Isle (Sir Henry Loch and Spencer Walpole). Mrs Fawcett also addressed concerns over the impact of suffrage on the feminine character, stating that they were not urging women to be less womanly, but to use their abilities and instincts to urge the state to improve the lot of those women who were not well off and to benefit the country at large.

At the end of the meeting, Mr H.A. Adamson moved that the meeting approve the appeal for women's suffrage and pledged itself to further the cause within Tynemouth. The resolution was seconded by Mrs Patterson and passed resoundingly.

The women of Northumberland, although many were mired in tradition, were nevertheless more than capable of seeing a better future for themselves and were, demonstrably, increasingly willing to fight for a cause which they believed would improve their lot.

CHAPTER TWO

The Edwardian Era:
Struggle and Suffrage

The Co-operative Women's Guild continued its expansion through Northumberland with a branch opening at Cramlington in November 1901. The expansion was driven by the example of the success of the guild on urban Tyneside and it fell to Mrs McBain of the Wallsend Branch (and secretary of the northern section of the guild) to formally open the branch with the support of another member of the Wallsend Branch, Mrs West, and one from Newcastle, Mrs Harbottle. The first meeting approved the officers and committee for the branch with a Mrs Holland being appointed as president. The committee quickly agreed that meetings would be held every Thursday evening in the ante-room of the Co-operative Hall.

Signifying the interest in the guild, there was a large attendance at the meeting and a public tea was followed by a lantern lecture by Mrs McBain on the guild and its leaders. The lecture was very well received and focused on the aims and work of the guild thus far and, no doubt, touched on the subject of women's suffrage as the guild had become decidedly more interested in the matter since its founding in 1883 (as the Women's League for the Spread of Co-operation). Alongside the issue of suffrage would have been examples of the value of the co-operative movement and the relief that movement could bring to women. Under the leadership of new General Secretary of the Guild, Margaret Llewelyn Davies, the guild was beginning a process of rapid expansion and was broadening its campaign beyond the issue of the co-operative movement, which was becoming more politically active in issues such as suffrage, women's health, the establishment of maternity benefits and of minimum wages.

The first years of the century saw a huge increase in interest in and support for women's suffrage throughout Northumberland. During the period, numerous branches of the various organizations campaigning for this cause arose in the county. In 1908, a branch of the NUWSS (National Union of Women's Suffrage Societies) was formed with Miss Ayre of 1 Howard Terrace as secretary (she was succeeded by a Miss McDowell of East Collingwood) although, despite the town's later links with the radical suffragettes, no local branch of the WSPU (Women's Social and Political Union) was ever set up in Morpeth. This was followed a year later by the forming of an NUWSS branch at Wansbeck (with Miss Pindar of Deleval Road, Whitley Bay and Mrs Baird of New Hurst, Ashington as joint secretaries, although they were succeeded by Mrs Tomlinson of Lilleville, Monkseaton in 1913). A branch was formed at Hexham (with a Mrs Wilkinson of Claremont, Westerhope as secretary) in 1910, while others were formed at Gosforth and Benton, Tynemouth, Shotley Bridge and Walker and Wallsend in succeeding years.

Northumbrian women were also becoming more interested as participants in sports. Tennis proved popular among many who could afford it and a number of lawn tennis clubs were inaugurated during the period. In November 1901, a lawn tennis club was formed in the village of Rothbury. Throughout the summer, enthusiasts of the sport had played a number of matches on the Rectory tennis courts at the invitation of Mr and Mrs Blackett-Ord and there was great enthusiasm about the formation of the club, which had both an adult and a junior section and was open to both men and women. By the end of the year, and showing the social status of many members, the club was in a very healthy financial situation with a balance of almost £14 being carried forward. The club was supported by Mr and Mrs Blackett and by Mrs Watson-Armstrong of

Cragside. A number of prizes were awarded yearly, including ones for mixed doubles and ladies' singles competitions.

However, the living conditions and lack of adequate medical care often left the women of Northumberland in dire circumstances. The strains of childbearing were a particular source of concern for many organizations such as the Co-operative Women's Guild. Infant mortality remained shockingly high, especially in working-class areas, and there was little treatment available for women who had suffered a traumatic birth culminating in the loss of a child. In March 1907, a typically tragic case was heard at Morpeth. The body of Mrs Sarah Arnot (27) of Collingwood Terrace, Morpeth had been pulled from the River Wansbeck above the George House Bridge. The inquest heard from Mr Arnot, a gardener and sergeant in the Volunteers, that his wife had given birth to their first child in November 1906, but that the child had lived only eight hours and that since this time Mrs Arnot had been very ill. In an effort to relieve her symptoms Mrs Arnot had gone to spend some time with her mother at Felton and had returned seemingly in a much better frame of mind, with Mr Arnot saying that she seemed to have benefited greatly from the break and that his wife was 'apparently in good spirits when she came home, and there had been no unpleasantness between them or anything to upset her in any way'.[1]

On the morning of Friday, 8 March Mr Arnot had breakfasted before setting out for work at around 9.35 am and had no idea that his wife was in anything but good spirits and he had no notion of what she intended. Mr Arnot had returned home at lunchtime, only to find the house deserted and no lunch prepared for him. At this, he became alarmed and went looking for her, only to discover that a body had been pulled from the river. Mr Arnot, under questioning from the coroner, testified that his wife had never given any indication of any intent to harm herself.

The body had been discovered by a Morpeth joiner named John William Wright. Mr Wright had been walking to work down the Mitford road when he saw a body lying in approximately 15in of water. He had immediately gone to inform the police in Morpeth. The reaction of Mr Wright resulted in some very firm criticism from the coroner. He was asked why had not attempted to pull the body from the water, especially as he had no way of knowing if the person was alive or not, and he answered only that he could not. The coroner expressed his disbelief and disgust at Mr Wright's conduct, telling him: 'Good Gracious! You, a man, and could not go into 15 or 16 inches of water and take the woman out! The woman might have been alive, and you might have saved her life. I never heard of such a thing.'[2] The coroner then asked if Mr Wright had been afraid and the witness admitted that he had been and that the discovery had completely unnerved him. The coroner, keen to chastise Mr Wright further, also criticized the fact that he did not return to the scene with the police, even though he was not asked to do so.

PC Helm gave evidence that he had been informed of the body by Mr Wright and had progressed immediately to the scene and had extricated the body of Mrs Arnot from the water, although he admitted that it had taken approximately half an hour to reach the scene. The police submitted into evidence several kind letters from her husband, which she had on her person and which had been written while she was at Felton. The coroner and jury returned a verdict that stated that Mrs Arnot had committed suicide while temporarily insane and that the 'poor woman, having gone through so much illness and trouble in the loss of her child, had under a sudden influence ended her life'.[3]

***

Although the suffrage movement found much support among a substantial percentage of the male population in Northumberland, not everyone agreed. Many of the meetings held by the suffragists were faced with vocal opposition and in a substantial number of cases young men attempted to storm the platforms upon which suffragists were speaking. One such case which occurred at Prudhoe in March 1907 resulted in court proceedings against three youths. The three – Thomas Porter, William Telfer and David Whitfield – were accused of having damaged furniture and fittings at the Drill Hall. The three had attended a suffragist meeting in company with a number of other youths, but had disagreed violently with the opinions expressed and the meeting had degenerated to the point at which it was suspended by Miss Fraser. Following this, the stage was rushed by a group of youths and damage was subsequently done to several chairs which were the property of the Drill Hall Company, Prudhoe. The secretary of the company testified that he had personally seen Whitfield and Telfer both break two chairs, while Porter had thrown a chair over the stage. Porter was contrite and apologized and was fined the sum of 5s and costs along with 3s 6d damages, while the other two were fined 10s plus costs and 7s damages.

Opposition towards not only women campaigning for the vote but also towards women playing any more active role in either work or public debate remained strong in many areas of society. The Duke of Northumberland was a vociferous critic of women involving themselves in matters which he saw as the traditional domain of men. Speaking in a debate in the House of Lords at the end of July 1907, he stated that he did not believe that women in Britain were increasing their influence through the 'modern fashion of engaging in these controversies and in work hitherto confined to men' and that the trend of women's interventions in public affairs created 'a diminution' in their traditional influence over their menfolk, which was based upon the fact that they did not experience the same 'influences which affected men'. Furthermore, he asserted: 'When the womanhood of England shrank from public appearances and public struggles with men they would be all the better and, not the worse, for the abstention.'

Needless to say, the suffragettes of Northumberland (and elsewhere) did not agree with His Grace's opinion and there were many criticisms of it in the local, national and specialist press. An article in *Women's Franchise*, for example, argued that the theory that women's influence over men was more effective when exerted indirectly was a fallacy that had been perpetrated by men so as to convince women that they should not become involved in public debate, while at the same time convincing them that their opinions held influence over men. The duke's argument that women's more active role in public affairs was a recent development was also queried, with the example of the influence over politics which, for example, abbesses had over Anglo-Saxon society and politics. Furthermore, argued the suffragettes, the pernicious issue of indirect influence was more open to abuse than the more direct methods that were being utilized by the suffragette movement.

For those women who found themselves having broken the law, drink was a common cause and the magistrates often looked very poorly upon women who were found to have committed crimes while under the influence of alcohol.

It was not only working-class women, however, who fell foul of the laws on drunkenness. A case at the end of August involved a Morpeth woman, Sarah Davis, described as being of very respectable appearance. Davis had bought a train ticket from Morpeth to Manchester and had approximately £2 10s in her purse when she alighted at Newcastle before going for a drink. She had then walked along Scotswood Road, believing she was making for Central Station, and some men who she did not know had given her some whisky. At approximately midnight Davis was found in a very drunken condition sitting on a step. Several men had attempted to carry her to a place of safety before the police arrived and the woman was taken to the station where she alleged that a wristwatch and her purse containing the money had gone missing. One of the men who had helped Davis was later charged with having stolen the watch and purse, while Davis was fined the sum of 5s plus costs for drunkenness.

One suffragette was to become synonymous with Northumberland: Emily Wilding Davison. In actual fact Emily was not a native Northumbrian, having been born in the London area, but her large family had had its background in Northumberland until very recently and the majority of her relatives were to be found living in the area around Morpeth, Northumberland. Her mother was a native of that county and could trace her roots back through Northumberland and into Scotland.

Emily and her siblings had been influenced throughout their childhood by the need for social reform. Emily's grandparents,

Davisons and Andersons, had been closely linked with some of the leading reforming politicians of their day. The Andersons, working for Earl Grey, had responsibility for attending to the extensive Fallodon and Howick estates during Earl Grey's lengthy absences. The Davisons had settled in the village of Milfield in north Northumberland where they had been influenced by the example of Josephine Elizabeth Butler (née Grey) who had been born in the village and was the daughter of a cousin of Earl Grey who had risen to be the reforming prime minister. Josephine had herself adopted a strong belief in social reform and the Davison siblings would have been made well aware of this aspect of their family history.

Emily's family history is rather convoluted. For example, both of her grandmothers were first cousins named Anderson. Elizabeth married a man named John Caisley who was variously described as a mining engineer, coal mine owner and publican of the White Swan in Newgate Street, Morpeth. Her sister Mary married a man named George Davison, a gun-maker whose first wife had died leaving him with five children. Mary was a notable gun-maker in her own right.[4]

Emily's father Charles had been a successful businessman in India and had married a wealthy heiress named Sarah Seton Chisholm in Simla in 1848 and the two had three sons while in India. The family moved back to Britain in 1854 and a year later a daughter was born at their home in London. The couple prospered in Britain and was even able to purchase property in Ireland in addition to their home in Warblington, Hampshire. The couple had four more children before Charles purchased Winton House in Dacre Street, Morpeth in 1863 and the family returned home to its Northumbrian roots.

In order to aid the Davisons settle into their new home, the many relatives who lived in the town and its hinterlands rallied round, with the Andersons and Caisleys all providing help. One of those who gave aid was Charles's young second cousin, Margaret Caisley. Margaret moved into Winton House in order to help with the children, while other relatives helped to care for Charles's now ailing wife.

Three years after the move north, the family had integrated into their new lives and Charles and his wife agreed to become guardians to a young girl, Jessie, who had been left orphaned after the death of her father, Major Corfield, in India. The family raised the young girl as one of their own family and Margaret Caisley played a significant role in helping her settle into her new surroundings.

In the same year, however, Charles's wife died (becoming the first of the family to be buried at Morpeth), and the greater part of the burden of looking after the family fell upon Margaret Caisley. Over the next two years Charles and Margaret appear to have grown ever closer and this developed into a rather unusual relationship between the widower and his young housekeeper. On 15 August 1868, Margaret gave birth to a daughter at Bar Moor in County Durham. The child, named Letitia Charlotte, was registered at first under the surname Dawson (a name associated with the Davison clan) before being baptized at Ryton as Letitia Charlotte Davison. Intriguingly, Charles gave his residence as being at Bath. Clearly the affair which had led to Letitia being conceived and born out of wedlock was somewhat scandalous. Various attempts have been made to try to explain it away as a normal relationship, but this was simply not the case.

At this time a child born out of wedlock was looked down upon by society and the relationship between Charles and Margaret featured an age gap which, even in that era, would have elicited comment. At the time of their marriage, months after the birth of their first daughter, Charles was aged 50 and Margaret just 19. That the couple seemed somewhat eager to obfuscate some aspects of their lives together adds to the suspicion that not everyone approved. We have as evidence for this the fact that Letitia was born away from Northumberland, Charles gave his address as Bath and, when the couple married, they did so not in Morpeth as might have been expected, but at the other end of the country at St Alphege, Greenwich, Kent. It is true that Charles conducted much of his business in the south of England and this could explain some of this, but the evidence, taken together, does appear to point to a wish to avoid scandal in Northumbrian society.

Nevertheless, Charles and Margaret continued to reside for a short time at Winton House and their second child, Alfred Norris Davison, was born there in May 1869 but, with his business interests in the south playing an ever larger role, Charles took the decision to place Winton House up for sale and to relocate the large family to Ealing, where they are mentioned as living in the 1871 census. It seems probable that at least one family member did not move, however, as a daughter named Sarah seems to have lived at Winton House for several years after the move, before marrying and settling in Dacre Cottage in Morpeth in 1875.

The family continued to live in the London area and on 11 October 1872 another daughter was born at Roxburgh House, 13 Vanbrugh Park Road, Greenwich. This daughter was named Emily Wilding Davison.

Emily's childhood was relatively prosperous and she is said to have enjoyed music, languages and sport and to have had a strong sense of faith. The family maintained an interest in social reform and in the interests of those who were on the bottom rung of society's ladder. One of Emily's half-brothers, William Seton Davison, recalled both Letitia and Emily accompanying their mother on her errands to deliver food parcels to the soup kitchens in London's East End. The parcels were distributed mainly to dockworkers' families and it is notable that when Emily's funeral cortège wound its way through London years later, those who attempted to jeer were often shouted down by groups of dockers.

At the beginning of May 1879, the family once more relocated, this time to a development built for those with connections to India at Riverdale Road, Twickenham. The move proved to be the first step in a series of misfortunes to bedevil the family. The house was poorly built and polluted with sewage and this led to the death of Emily's youngest sister Ethel. Charles took the builders to court but lost his case, although the family was permitted to resign the lease on the property. Charles lost money in this case and this was exacerbated by a series of bad moves through investments in various tram companies and in his attempts as an inventor.

Emily was well educated, having attended Kensington High School for Girls where she established a reputation as a very able student with a particular propensity towards art, literature and languages. By 1891 Emily was attending Holloway College, but early the following year her sister Amy was divorced from her husband in what became a very messy and costly court case. This further denuded the family fortunes and adversely affected Charles Davison's health. The experience of the case also probably played a role in furthering Emily's interests in women's place in society, especially with regard to women being able to own their own property.

On 7 February 1893, Charles Davison died and the family was forced to move out of their home in Kensington. Charles left just £102 in his will (just shy of £13,000 today) and it rapidly became clear that the family would have to rein in their spending. Emily, however, was packed off to college by her mother who was determined that her daughter should continue her education if at all possible. Emily was keenly aware of the sacrifice this would be and was very worried about her mother and siblings. She wrote to relatives in Morpeth at this time expressing her worries as her college cost £20 per term and she was determined that this money must not be wasted. As it was, she later had to withdraw from the college due to a lack of funds.

Emily and her family had maintained links with their Northumbrian relatives, and this was to prove crucial in Margaret's decision to move back to Northumberland in order to open her own bakery and confectioners at Longhorsley.

The family business interests included, as we have seen, not only gun-makers but also mine owners. By the mid-1870s the Caisley family were owners of several pits in Northumberland including two near Rothbury, and it was here, in 1874, that three of Emily's first cousins were born. One highlighted again to Emily the injustices suffered by women in Britain. Jessie May (known as Mamie) Caisley was born at Bushy Gap near Rothbury to

Dorothy Caisley. The child was born out of wedlock but was not as fortunate as Emily's sister Letitia had been. Dorothy was working in service to the titled family of the Hodges of Newcastle-upon-Tyne and she had been made pregnant by Robert Trotter Hermon-Hodge, the then 23-year-old son of the house. Jessie was not, at the time of her birth, acknowledged but Hermon-Hodge did provide some care for his illegitimate child, albeit in a callous manner. It was said that he would ride past the Caisleys' house and throw a couple of sovereigns over the hedge for the support of Jessie before riding on without further acknowledgement.[5] The experiences of Jessie, who was a favourite of Emily's, undoubtedly contributed to her growing determination to see change for the women of Britain.

It is not known exactly when Margaret relocated to Longhorsley, but by 1895 the family's Irish estate had been sold and Letitia married a dashing French ship's broker named Frederick Charles de Baecker in December of that year and the couple left to set up home, in some luxury, at St Malo where Emily was invited to spend Christmas and the New Year. The family fortunes were still somewhat precarious, but had recovered enough for Emily to attend St Hugh's College, Oxford, in order to take her exams. Emily obtained a 1st Class (Honours) award in English Language and Literature in 1895, but the award was not given as Oxford did not at that time confer degrees on women. A tale has circulated about how Emily celebrated her degree by going onto the village green at Longhorsley and throwing sweets into the air for the local children to catch.[6]

Emily was forced to find work and settled into a life as a governess to the Moorhouse family at Spratton, Northamptonshire. This was probably not the most challenging job for a woman such as Emily, but no doubt inspired by her mother's example, she performed well. During this period she may also have been influenced to some degree by the attitude of the mistress of the Moorhouse household towards women and the vote. Mrs Mary Anne Moorhouse (née Rhodes) was a New Zealander and the fact that the women of New Zealand had been granted both the vote and full citizenship may have been discussed from time to time.[7]

Although Emily remained with the Moorhouse family for only a short period, this was undoubtedly a formative time in her life. Stripped of the relative comfort of her former life, Emily was, for the first time, forced to confront a future in which she would have to depend upon her own efforts to maintain herself. It was not only in the field of employment where Emily's life had radically changed. With little prospect now of any substantial dowry, Emily's chances of a prosperous marriage match receded significantly and it would seem that Emily realized that any chance of future prosperity or a sense of self-respect might rely more on education, work and, later on, the esteem of colleagues in the suffrage movement.

Over the next few years, Emily continued working as a governess, notably in the household of Sir Francis Layland-Barratt MP, while continuing her studies. It seems clear that during this period of her life Emily was struggling to forge a purpose for herself and that she was missing her relatives in Northumberland. Numerous postcards and letters from this period are addressed to her Northumbrian relatives, swapping news of events.

Despite her financial circumstances, Emily still seems to have been able to travel, largely with the Layland-Barratt family, and in April 1905 she departed for a holiday to Florence. Very possibly she stopped off on the way to visit her sister Letitia in Paris and she visited the statue of Joan of Arc. Throughout her life Emily looked upon St Joan as an inspiration and she encouraged other young women to learn of her. The Morpeth-born suffragette Isabella Thompson Atkinson described to her daughters how Emily had sent her a signed book about the life of Joan of Arc. Emily spent Christmas 1905 with her sister but, intriguingly, there is a gap in the frequent correspondence between Emily and her family between this point and the resumption of letters in early 1907 (it is believed she left the employ of the Layland-Barratt family at the end of 1905). Were letters from this period among those burned by her mother shortly before Margaret's death? It was in the landmark year of 1906 that Emily took the decision to join the WSPU, following meetings with several members in and around the Salford area. Emily was still employed as a governess, but now she also accompanied her charges as a chaperone to various Liberal meetings and was further exposed to Liberal policies of reform and social change (even though the party did not yet completely support women's suffrage). During her final years of employment as a teacher and governess, Emily had become increasingly aware of the need for social reform and of the various issues which adversely affected the lives of many women in Britain.

Emily remained in contact with her relatives in Northumberland throughout 1907 and was particularly concerned with the wellbeing of Gladys Wilkinson who had recently left her home in Morpeth to take up the post of companion housekeeper and shop assistant to Emily's mother in Longhorsley. Gladys was the latest in a long line of Wilkinson daughters to have undertaken this role which seems to have been almost a family tradition.

Of Emily's earliest involvement with the WSPU, little has been revealed but it is known that in September 1907 she was in Edinburgh for a time and, as the WSPU was at that time organizing a substantial campaign in Scotland, it is more than likely that Emily was part of the administrative organization of this campaign.

In 1908, the WSPU organized a huge demonstration in London's Hyde Park which would culminate in a meeting at the Albert Hall. By this time Emily had been a member for eighteen months and she was entrusted with the position of steward for the Marylebone Station section of the demonstration. Emily was present at the suffragette pageant when 66,000 women marched through London dressed as historical figures. It was in response to campaigns such as these and the relative lack of movement they inspired in politicians that Emily began to become more and more convinced that radical action was the only means through which women would succeed in obtaining the vote.

By 1908, Emily was becoming increasingly active within the movement and her increasing involvement with and dedication to the WSPU was causing a strain between her personal beliefs and her career as a teacher. It is more than likely that growing friction and tension had caused Emily to depart from the teaching post she had held for several years and go to work as a private tutor. Another reason for the change was that the move brought her closer to the activities of the WSPU as she swapped remote country life for the metropolis. Throughout Emily's life she longed for the London life which she had known, but balanced this with a love of the rugged and peaceful countryside of Northumberland. Like many facets of her life, this dichotomy has puzzled those who have sought to assess Emily's character and motivations.

Although Morpeth was to become intimately linked with the radical suffragette movement through its connections to Emily Davison, the town was actually far more committed to the non-radical suffragist movement, and the town council and many of the prominent members of society in and around Morpeth were supporters of the cause, but preferred more peaceful means of attaining their aims.

In February 1909, the Wansbeck Women's Liberal Association held its annual meeting at Morpeth Town Hall. Mrs Molly Trevelyan, the wife of Sir Charles Trevelyan MP and then Parliamentary Secretary to the Board of Education, of nearby Wallington Hall was to have presided over the meeting but was suffering from a sore throat and therefore sent a written address to be read to the assembly.[8]

At the beginning of her address Mrs Trevelyan informed the audience that her mother-in-law, Lady Trevelyan, wished the members well, praised the work that they had performed that year and urged them to be ready to push the suffrage question and to support local politicians such as Mr Burt and Mr Fenwick. The address reinforced this by stating that the greatest reform required by women was that of suffrage and that those who believed in the cause must be ready to oppose the newly formed and expanding Women's National Anti-Suffrage League (WNASL) whose membership included 'many able women' and was attempting, through its expansion throughout the country, to oppose the vote being given to women. Mrs Trevelyan had good cause to be wary of the abilities of the WNASL as her half-sister, the famed traveller, archaeologist, political advisor and sometime secret agent Gertrude Bell, was a founder member of the league and president of the northern section. Not only was Gertrude an anti-suffrage campaigner, but so were her parents.

Despite this family split, Mrs Trevelyan declared that she was not afraid of their opponents, describing their arguments as feeble, being founded on the belief that women were capable of expressing a political opinion but not of enforcing it in a physical manner and that therefore they could not be permitted to play a voting role in a general election. Mrs Trevelyan also argued that women would be able to influence the working conditions experienced by thousands of married women across the country and that this could only lead to a healthier future. Mrs Trevelyan argued that the final argument of all anti-suffragists was that such a thing had not been done before but stated that this was no argument at all, and if this argument had been accepted then the human race would never have progressed in any manner. Mrs Trevelyan's remarks were well received by the audience and the reading of her address was frequently interrupted by applause or cheering.

In the absence of Mrs Trevelyan, the main speaker was Miss Alison Garland, a prominent member of the Women's National Liberal Foundation (WNLF). Miss Garland was also a committed suffragist, an active member of the NUWSS and of the Women's Liberals Forward Suffrage Union.[9] Despite a heavy cold, Miss Garland gave a witty and vigorous speech. Early in her speech Miss Garland stated that the Liberal government had done much good, but had been stymied on numerous occasions by the House of Lords. This she decried and stated that in her opinion, women would do a much better job of opposing the Upper House than had been demonstrated by the men in the House of Commons. This opinion was met with loud and sustained cheers.

The majority of Miss Garland's speech, however, was of a far more wide-ranging political nature. When talking about the Old Age Pensions Act, she stated that this was of great interest to women as far more women lived to a greater age than did men, before stating that the best way to get an extension to the Act was to keep the current Liberal government in power. She then demonstrated her political bias by referring to the recent by-election which had been held in Newcastle the previous year. This had seen a substantial swing that resulted in the Conservatives, whose candidate was George Renwick, gaining the seat from the Liberals. Demonstrating some callousness, Miss Garland stated that she could not understand those who had voted for the Conservatives and that she 'would like to cut such people off with a shilling.... They don't deserve pensions.'[10]

Perhaps aware that her line was not soliciting great enthusiasm, Miss Garland then changed tack to once more focus on gender matters. She stressed that female Liberals were urging women's suffrage in a constitutional manner and added that this was only fair as women did not try to define the role of men as men did with women.

The Wansbeck Women's Liberal Association was, at the time, in a healthy state with 344 members. A separate association had also recently been founded at Seaton Delaval. The meeting concluded with a vote being passed that urged the government of Mr Asquith to make women's suffrage a clause of the proposed Reform Bill.

By early 1909, aged 36, Emily had taken the decision to abandon teaching to dedicate herself solely to activism in the name of the movement. By March she had become a trusted part of the WSPU and was moving on from undertaking administrative tasks to taking the more active role that she sought. Selected as part of a delegation to the prime minister, she attempted to force a petition into the hands of Mr Asquith in what was her first real act of militancy. Appearing in court for the offence, she was offered the chance to redeem herself by giving an undertaking to stop attending such deputations. This tempting offer, made because Emily was previously of good character with no criminal record, was refused outright by this increasingly determined and dedicated woman. Clearly Emily was unafraid of the consequences of gaining a criminal record;

a clear sign of her growing determination to aid the movement by whatever means were necessary. Emily was instead sentenced to one month in prison. This willingness to gain a criminal record and go to prison for the cause gained Emily further influence within the movement and she was increasingly recognized as playing a progressively important role in the campaign within the capital. Her dedication and influence, however, went far beyond London and extended increasingly into Northumberland.

During her periods of imprisonment, Emily sought strength from her belief in the cause for which she was suffering and from her belief that what the suffragettes were fighting for was not only a political struggle but also one of faith. During one spell in prison Emily was heartened, as she reported to the newspaper *Votes for Women*, to find an inscription on the wall reading *Dum spiro spero* ('While I breathe, I hope') which had been left by Mrs Dove-Willcox. She related how she had left her own contribution below the original, reading: 'Rebellion against tyrants is obedience to God.'[11]

A meeting was held in Morpeth by the National Women's Social and Political Union on the last day of August, Emily being the main speaker. The local newspaper, however, while being generally supportive of the cause, remained doubtful of the tactics being employed by members of the WSPU such as Emily. An article, one of a regular series in the paper entitled 'Our Own Column' (written by 'Ourselves'), covering the meeting admitted that Emily gave an eloquent defence of the extreme tactics and of the cause, but that such methods had undoubtedly prejudiced local opinion and had alienated the cause from a surge of sympathy which it would otherwise have found. The article then went on to describe as ludicrous the arguments of the Women's Anti-Suffrage League (WASL), that the people of Britain were now bored with the issue, and admitted that the activities of the suffragettes, in attracting media attention and arousing public debate, positive or negative, had the result of keeping the issue firmly in the forefront of the minds of the public. In the opinion of the reporter, the best part of Emily's speech on that night was when she reminded the listeners of the violence of men in campaigning for the franchise and other political reforms and concluded that the 'uppermost impression made on one's mind by this educated and cultured lady's earnest address was that no power will be long able to withstand an agitation persistently carried on by a body of such able enthusiasts'.[12]

Despite Emily's claim that the tactics of the suffragettes were not violent but political in nature she, along with four companions, was imprisoned in Manchester after they had been found guilty of throwing metal balls (almost hysterically referred to as 'bombs' by the press) onto the glass roof of a meeting hall in which the Chief Secretary for Ireland, Augustine Birrell, was speaking on the subject of the budget. Magistrates had given the five women the option to pay fines, but they had refused and had instead been imprisoned in Strangeways. The five immediately went on hunger strike and were found guilty of having broken prison regulations, therefore they were placed in punishment cells. Once again, the 'Our Own Column' put forward a rather acerbic opinion stating that those who had attended Miss Davison's recent meeting would no doubt remember her assertions that the struggle of the suffragettes was a political one and not violent, before snidely commenting that 'Bomb-throwing, we may suppose, is one of the manifestations of high politics.'[13]

Clearly, even among the local press, both the campaign for women's suffrage and the methods used by the suffragettes, as opposed to those of the suffragists, continued to strongly divide opinion and the debate was growing ever more rancorous. It cannot be denied, however, that the subject was one that continually attracted and focused the attention of the public, with the result that the cause was seldom out of the news.

One of the more unusual links to emerge from the suffrage campaign in Northumberland was that between the local suffragists and the Italian revolutionary Giuseppe Garibaldi. A mariner, Garibaldi had travelled extensively to and from Tyneside with cargoes of coal and when his ship was docked at Tynemouth he had engaged in debates with the local coal mine owners and radical reformers who were based in the north of

England. Garibaldi was himself to become a firm supporter of women's suffrage and, in gratitude for his support, the suffragists raised funds for his proposed reforms in his home country.

With her fame, or perhaps infamy among some quarters, cemented locally from the period of imprisonment in Holloway and, more recently, in Strangeways Gaol, Manchester, having been charged in connection with the 'bomb'-throwing incident at the meeting held by Mr Birrell, it is perhaps unsurprising that local supporters of the cause were anxious to give a rousing welcome to Emily Davison when she returned home. Led by Mrs Taylor of Chipchase Castle, Miss Williams and Miss C. Brown, the local members of the WSPU made special arrangements for Emily's arrival at Morpeth Market Square on Saturday, 18 September 1909.

In the afternoon, before Emily's arrival, a meeting was held in the square with speeches given by Mrs Taylor and Miss Williams, at the culmination of which the assembled crowd was invited to accompany them to the station to greet Emily's arrival. The parade to the station was headed by a brass band followed by the above-named ladies in a brake. They were followed by members and supporters of the WSPU bearing a number of banners with various slogans upon them, notably 'Votes for Women' and 'Welcome Northumbrian Hunger-Striker'.

Upon her arrival at the station, Emily was escorted to a carriage drawn by two horses and was taken 'in state' to the Market Place, followed by the brake which was now fully occupied by suffragists. Upon her arrival at the Market Place a large crowd had gathered and Mrs Taylor presided over a further meeting at which Emily addressed the crowd, describing her experiences during her four-day hunger strike while in Strangeways. She 'received a patient and sympathetic hearing'. In her speech, Emily commented that in the time since she had last addressed a meeting in the Market Place just over a fortnight previously she had suffered much, only to recover and, with a reassuring smile, added she had recovered to re-join her 'brave comrades in the firing line'.[14]

Emily then reassured the crowd, telling them that theirs was a political struggle and methods employed were not violent, but that in recent times they had been caused to advance their strategies due to the fault of the current government whose 'obstinacy would not read the signs of the times'. She described how some women had been convicted of throwing stones and other items, but told them that such measures had only been taken as a response to the ongoing budget campaign which, as everyone knew, would affect women as much as anyone else and that it was, therefore, frustrating that women were kept out of the debate and denied access to meetings discussing the matter.[15] She asked the men in the crowd how they would react if they turned up to such a meeting, only to be told by stewards that they would not be allowed access or, if they were, would not be permitted to ask any questions. She assumed that they would react with anger and would force their way into the meeting. Well, Emily argued, women had not the physical force of men and so had been obliged to use other methods such as that at Manchester when she had thrown a metal ball (with the message 'Votes for Women' wrapped around it) through a window into the hall where the meeting was taking place.

Once more she told the crowd that it was the fault of the government that suffragists had been forced to take more serious action, before saying that it would be their fault if they were compelled to take even more desperate measures and assuring the crowd that neither she nor her comrades would flinch if this were the case. Continuing in her political vein, Emily told the crowd that the one great obstacle to the cause was none other than Mr Asquith himself and that the Liberals should live up to their promises to support reform.

Emily then turned to a description of her time in Strangeways, describing the prison as being a peculiarly 'very clean and well-kept prison'. Everyone at the prison, she said, had treated her and her companions with sympathy, with the exception of the governor. She described how she and her companions had made their familiar protest, telling the authorities that if they were treated as first-class prisoners they would obey the prison regulations, but if they were treated as second-class they would refuse. Emily described how she had immediately been thrown into a punishment cell which featured only a plank bed fastened to the wall and a tree-trunk chained to the wall upon which to sit (oddly, the crowd laughed at this point), and that the window was not free to open. Emily argued that there 'was no need to cause consumption among the prisoners by shutting them up' in such cells and described how she had spent her first night trying to break the window to let in air (at this point the crowd cried out 'Hear, hear').[16] She succeeded in breaking the window early in the morning, only for the matron to come in and tell her, apologetically, that the magistrates had given instructions that any prisoner who broke their window should be handcuffed. This done, Emily described how she had been kept handcuffed in her cell all the time with no opportunity for exercise, but that at least those who had broken their windows could hear the words of their companions outside who were holding meetings to support them. At the conclusion of the meeting, three cheers were given for Emily and for Miss Brown, who was also a former hunger-striker.

In the same edition of the newspaper in which the above account of the return of Emily was given, there appeared a letter from Emily on the subject of women's suffrage. She began by expressing the hope that her words at the meeting in the Market Place had convinced 'many Laodicean friends' of the cause (once again showing her erudition, as Laodicean means half-hearted) of the reasons for the change to more extreme tactics. She believed that men had, perhaps, no right to criticize the tactics employed by women, as a Mr Joseph John Hills of Newbiggin had avowed in an earlier letter to the newspaper. Despite this, she wrote, she still felt that there were many people within the district who needed a further explanation. She expressed the opinion that the simple reason was that the government was to blame by causing further offence to those who already had more than sufficient cause for dissatisfaction in their treatment. She described the government as goading women 'by unconstitutional action by using force to hold them back from their just right of petition and of free access to so-called "public meetings" on great public questions' and that, if this was so, then the blame surely lay with the government 'which hides its head in the sand like an ostrich and refuses to observe the signs of the times'.[17]

The cause of women's suffrage continued to give rise to harsh divisions of opinion within Northumberland. Immediately below Emily's letter was one from a J. Horne of Hazlerigg that gave a far harsher view of the tactics employed by suffragettes such as Emily. Horne was replying to the letter from Mr Hills and he began by asserting that using violent tactics was a poor example and demonstrated a lack of self-control. He concluded his first paragraph by saying that those women who felt that the best way to express their opinions was to chain themselves to railings, slap the faces of policemen, break up public meetings and 'behave generally like deranged lunatics' was not to be praised but decried as a poor example. Horne continued by saying that he would like to see the government put forward a Bill for women's suffrage only for it to be rejected by the House of Lords because it would be amusing to see 'these pampered daughters of plutocrats supporting the Liberal Party against their brothers and cousins'. He went on to say that he had some experience of public meetings and that in every one any man or woman who wished to express an opinion or ask a question was heard with 'the utmost courtesy and civility, but the behaviour of these distinguished ladies is, to say the least of it, barbarous, disgusting and most discreditable'. Somewhat incredulously, he then asserted that 'Hard-working women don't care a fig about the Franchise.' Having decried the actions of the suffragettes, Mr Horne then went on to say that he was in fact an ardent supporter of the elective franchise because he believed that the majority of working women would 'vote progressive, and so accelerate reform'.[18]

Emily was, by this stage, clearly determined in her belief that direct action was absolutely necessary to draw attention to her cause and was left unabashed and unmoved by her recent experiences with the law. Always a committed and determined woman, she was, by now, utterly convinced of the righteousness of her actions and was determined to see them through. Just weeks after she had appeared in Morpeth Market Square, she was once again in court, charged with having disrupted a political meeting and having broken windows. This occasion demonstrated clearly that Emily was more than prepared to take militant action wherever the opportunity arose.

On Saturday, 9 October, the Chancellor, David Lloyd George, visited Newcastle and the local suffragette movement undertook a series of militant protests designed to draw attention to their cause. Shortly after midnight, four suffragettes were arrested for breaking several windows at the Liberal Club, valued at £3 7s 6d. The four – Violet Bryant (26), Ellen Pitfield (44), Lily Asquith (25) and Dorothy Shellard (29) – were brought before magistrates the same morning and all, despite the fact that none of them had legal representation, acknowledged their guilt, with Pitfield stating that she threw the stone in cold blood as a blow against the government. Some of the other women attempted to argue their cause, but they were cut short by the chairman and sentenced to fourteen days' hard labour.

With the police already anticipating trouble, barricades were set up in and around the areas where the chancellor was to be and, later in the morning, there were further disturbances. One suffragette, Winifred Jones (32) of 19 Nixon Street, Newcastle, eluded the significant police presence and managed to break a window at the Palace Theatre and there were disturbances on the streets near the barricades. Around the Barras Bridge area some women suspected of being suffragettes were 'hustled rather severely in the congested streets' by a hostile crowd with a few taking 'shelter in shops' or escaping on tramcars, but several more remained steadfast in their determination to make their protest. Three women were arrested near the barriers. A Mrs Brailsford (the wife of a prominent London journalist) was arrested making an attack on a barricade with a hatchet, while Lady Constance Lytton was arrested for throwing a stone which was said to have narrowly missed the mother of Mr Walter Runciman. The final arrest here was that of Emily, who was apprehended in the act of throwing a stone, which had a label attached reading: 'To Lloyd George. Rebellion against tyrants is obedience to God. Deeds, not words.'[19]

Later that night there was a concerted attack on several Post Offices in Newcastle and damage was caused at a number of sites. Four suffragettes were arrested during these attacks. They were Miss Dorothy Pothick, Miss Kitty Marion, Miss Kathleen Brown and Miss Ellen Pitman. A total of twelve suffragettes were arrested during the day and the police boasted that Mr Lloyd George had neither seen nor heard any of the protests. It was also revealed that one suffragette attempted to bribe the attendant at the Palace Theatre with 2s if he would let her hide on the roof until the chancellor arrived.

Once again Emily remained undeterred, despite the physical and mental punishment that repeated spells of imprisonment were inflicting upon her. She continued her militant campaign with a further window-breaking attack. This time she appeared in front of magistrates at Bury on 26 October. The charges related to her, along with Catherine Tolson of Hale in Cheshire, Hannah Shepherd of Rochdale and Helen Gordon Liddle of Peaslake in Surrey (all described as committed suffragettes), having broken windows at the Radcliffe Liberal Club, where Mr Runciman was addressing a meeting, and at Radcliffe Post Office. The women were all fined the sum of £2, but, once again, they refused to pay.

Motivated in part by the petition for women's suffrage which now had more than 250,000 signatures, Asquith agreed to give the Conciliatory Bill of 1910 parliamentary time. This Bill, if enacted into law, would see approximately 1,000,000 women who owned property over the value of £10 receive the vote. The Newcastle Branch of the NUWSS voted in favour of the Bill and encouraged other north-east branches to do the same. At the same time, a campaign of open-air meetings was arranged throughout the area. Meetings were held throughout June at a number of Northumbrian towns and villages including North Shields and Morpeth. At the latter town, Miss Mein and Miss Edith Ericsson explained the new Bill to a 200-strong meeting in the Market Place and urged the townsfolk to vote in favour so as to show their appreciation of the efforts of local MP Mr Burt, who was a member of the Conciliation Committee, in his support for the cause of women's suffrage. The resolution was carried with only two dissenting votes.

As it happened the vote was successful, despite many suffragists opposing it as it would deny the vote to many women, but the Bill never made it into law as the General Election intervened. This resulted in hundreds of suffragists marching on parliament.

By April 1910, Emily was being paid by the WSPU and she was throwing herself with ever greater dedication and fervour into the cause. In 1911, she made her way into the ventilation shafts of the House of Commons before hiding in the crypt and then a cupboard in order to avoid the census and, it was believed, to interrupt a sitting of the House. Emily later wrote to the *Morpeth Herald* saying that as a result of her protest she had been registered twice, once at her lodgings in Coram Street and once in the Houses of Parliament.

The campaign to avoid the census found great favour with many suffragists and supporters of the cause and significant disruption was caused. Acts included avoiding the census and in giving false information. Northumbrian-born suffragist and reformer Josephine Butler, for example, stated that she had been born on Flodden Field, Scotland, and this was duly recorded despite the fact that Josephine had in fact been born at Milfield in north Northumberland and that Flodden Field itself does not lie in Scotland but in Northumberland.

During this period in her life Emily was sentenced to various terms in prisons across the country, and force-feeding and imprisonment in extremely poor conditions had a severely deleterious effect upon her health. When released from her various terms of imprisonment, Emily spent short periods of time recuperating either with her mother at Longhorsley or with William Seton Davison and his wife Sarah. William had a medical background and this aided in her recovery, but the care of the couple came at a cost as they were often vilified and their children even had to change their names at school.

Later in 1911 Emily, along with Charlotte Marsh, was arrested while breaking windows in Regent Street and then, in

November, Emily was re-arrested for setting fire to a number of letterboxes. This was something of a watershed moment in Emily's activism as she had undertaken the action on her own initiative without the permission or connivance of the WSPU and this would lead to something of a breakdown in her relationship with several of the leaders of the WSPU. The actions that Emily had taken during her mission to set fire to letterboxes resulted in the imposition of a jail sentence of six months in December. During this sentence Emily again undertook a hunger strike and was forcibly fed with great brutality. It was during this sentence that Emily seems to have become somewhat despondent, and this in turn led to her growing conviction that women would never receive the vote until a suffragette became a martyr in a move that would shock the nation into action. Spurred on by this growing conviction, Emily determined on a suicide attempt during which she threw herself deliberately from a staircase in the prison.[20]

As a result of her actions, Emily was left seriously hurt with severe head, back, shoulder and neck injuries. Regardless of this, the authorities left her more or less untreated for some time and even force-fed Emily despite her injuries. This brutal treatment resulted in extremely severe pain for Emily and demonstrated a brutality which angered many of her fellow suffragettes in the prison.

On 12 September 1912, Emily gave an address at Morpeth Market Place. Her speech was heavily influenced by the struggles of the previous three years and she began by telling her audience of the changes that had taken place since she had addressed a similar meeting at Morpeth in 1909. Since then, she argued, things had changed markedly. She described how the radical campaign had been scaled back while the Conciliation Bill was before parliament, but that once that Bill had been killed off, largely through the efforts of Mr Asquith and Mr Churchill, according to Emily, then the suffragette movement had once more had to embark on a radical campaign and had, indeed, been forced to adopt ever more radical methods. The government response to this was to imprison suffragettes and to impose harsh treatment upon them amounting to torture. Emily related how, at that very moment, two of her friends were in prison and experiencing force-feeding. Emily added that for 'refined women suffering imprisonment for conscience sake forcible feeding was nothing less than torture'.[21]

The account in the local press does not give any information about the size of the crowd or the reaction of those who were in the Market Place. This seems somewhat unusual. Emily was not, despite the accounts given by the local press previously, noted as a particularly effective speaker, but her activities had given her a notoriety in the area and her upbringing and very extensive family connections in the Morpeth area meant that she enjoyed a great deal of sympathy and it is likely that there was a substantial crowd.

Morpeth continued to host a number of meetings dedicated to the cause of women's suffrage. On 16 September 1912, a large meeting was held in the town hall under the auspices of the North-Eastern Federation of Women's Suffrage Societies. The keynote speaker at the meeting was to have been Dr Ethel Williams, the first female doctor in Newcastle, but she was unavoidably detained and her place taken by Miss Gordon. Dr Williams was a supporter of women's suffrage who was not noted at this point for militancy, but she had recently refused to pay her taxes until the fate of the Conciliation Bill was known and this stance had attracted considerable attention and praise from local suffragists.

In October 1912, Emily and her comrade, Miss Laura Ainsworth, met with the MP for Wansbeck Division, Mr Charles Fenwick, at the Burt Hall, Newcastle, to discuss the issue of women's suffrage. Emily and Laura had worked together after Miss Ainsworth worked with the WSPU in Newcastle in 1911. The two had collaborated closely in the efforts to evade the census of 1911 and had much in common, with Miss Ainsworth being a prominent militant who had been force-fed after being arrested with Mary Leigh and Charlotte Marsh in 1909. At the meeting, Mr Fenwick told the two militant suffragettes that he had been a supporter of women's suffrage ever since he had been returned to parliament in 1885. He stated that he would support the Reform Bill, but would give no guarantees to vote against the third reading if the amendments to include women were not approved by the House. Mr Fenwick also condemned the actions of the more militant members of the suffragist movement, telling the two militants that these methods had damaged the cause significantly. In reply to this, the two suffragettes put it to Mr Fenwick that no such cause as theirs had ever won without strenuous efforts on the part of its members and that they were fully justified in their actions due to the government's intransigence. They also defended their actions by comparing them to those of the miners and those of the Chartists, but Mr Fenwick bluntly told them that 'he did not regard these cases as at all analogous'.[22]

The National Union of Women's Suffrage Societies (NUWSS) continued to hold meetings across Northumberland with meetings at both Hexham and Morpeth in January 1913. Many of these meetings showcased the numerous social causes which members of the NUWSS were active or interested in aside from the question of women's suffrage. On 7 January, a drawing-room meeting was held in the home of Mrs E. Browne, Rochwood, Elvaston Road, Hexham, which was very well attended, with approximately sixty people present. The main subject for this meeting was a talk on white slavery by a Miss Hare of Brighton. According to the speaker, the main causes for this trade were bad housing conditions, inadequate lodging-house accommodation and sweated labour in the cities of Britain. These social evils, argued Miss Hare, combined to aggravate the evil of white slave-trafficking. The meeting was presided over by the Reverend Ellis Pearson and in thanking Miss Hare for her 'courageous speech', expressed himself as 'in the closest sympathy with the women's movement' and with the opinions that had been expressed by Miss Hare.[23] Eight days later, the Morpeth Branch of the NUWSS held a meeting at which it discussed the future work of the branch and welcomed nine new members who had joined in December 1912.

The meetings of members of the NUWSS were held very regularly and demonstrated the support for the society in many areas of Northumberland. A further drawing-room meeting was held in Morpeth on 29 January. The venue, once again, shows support for the cause with Canon Davies, the rector of Morpeth, loaning the use of the St James Institute. Refreshments were supplied by Miss Hopper and there were thirty ladies in attendance. Miss Hopper, who presided over the meeting, first outlined the political history of the suffragist movement over the previous two years and 'summed up the present critical position of affairs' before turning the floor over to the chosen speaker for the meeting, Mrs Abbott. In her speech, Mrs Abbott urged every member of the society to rededicate themselves to the cause and to show their resolve through ever greater loyalty to the leaders of the society. At the conclusion of the meeting a resolution was carried unanimously for the government to enfranchise women. The meeting once again was met with enthusiasm and four new members were enrolled, bringing the number in the Morpeth Branch to sixty.[24]

On 19 February, the Hexham Branch held its annual meeting at which it was revealed that seventeen meetings had been held over the course of 1912 and that the total membership of the branch at the end of 1912 had now reached ninety-four and that with six new enrolments at the annual meeting the total had reached the figure of 100. The meeting also heard how the branch had a deficit of £6 19s 3d and various posts were voted into place with Mrs Pumphrey (president), Mrs Walton (secretary), Miss Lowe (treasurer) and Mrs Graham-Thompson (press secretary) all being re-elected, as were members of the committee including Mrs Lamb and Mrs Harbottle of Corbridge, while Mrs Ridley of Haydon Bridge seconded the vote that new members should be enrolled. The speaker was Miss Beaver who gave an excellent address that considered the present political situation. Demonstrating the interest that was being maintained in the issue of women's suffrage, there were representatives from local newspapers the *Hexham Courant* and the *Hexham Herald* present to cover the meeting.

On 9 May, Miss Sheard of the Gosforth and Benton Branch of the NUWSS held a meeting at the home of Mrs Spence

(Melbreak, Gosforth) which resulted in the welcoming of eight new members to the society. The main speaker was a Miss Matters who chose as her subject 'The Inner Meaning of the Women's Movement' and her speech was said to have made a very deep and inspiring impression upon the audience.[25]

On 14 May, the South-East Wansbeck Branch held a meeting in the Schirley Lodge, Monkseaton home of Mrs Montgomery. The main speaker at the meeting was Norwegian suffragist Fru Anker, who attracted a large audience who warmly applauded her speech comparing the experiences of women in her home country with those in Britain.

The support of many prominent male members of Morpeth Town Council was a boost to the suffragist cause in the area and this was once again highlighted at a public meeting which took place in the town hall on 15 May 1913. The meeting was presided over by Mr F. Brumell and he was supported on the platform by the mayor (Alderman R.J. Carr), the rector Canon Davies, and the Reverend James Haworth. The support of these prominent Morpethian men, however, did come with some reservations as the chair made it clear from the outset of the meeting that their support for the NUWSS arose from the fact that it was a non-party and non-militant society. Mr Brumell went on to state that the militant actions of a small party of women claiming to act on behalf of the general cause was deplored by them and that such actions were 'injurious to the best interests of the cause they claimed to be assisting'.[26]

A highlight of the meeting was an address by the Norwegian journalist, author, women's rights campaigner and suffragist Fru Anker, who gave a speech on how Norwegian women had secured the vote in Norway and how they had subsequently used it. At the time Fru was involved in a lengthy speaking tour of Britain. The Norwegian suffragist went on to detail how a Norwegian woman had first demanded the vote at the time of the Napoleonic Wars and that this woman's granddaughter had gone on to become the first female Member of Parliament in Norway and how the work of John Stuart Mill had given impetus to the movement with the first suffrage union being formed in 1885. She then described how, through the patriotism they had shown during the crisis with Sweden some twenty years later, the women of Norway had won for themselves the vote. Perhaps eager to counter criticism from some British Liberal politicians that the majority of women would vote Conservative, Fru pointed out how in the two Norwegian elections in which women had voted, they had been on the side of reform. One of the amusing anecdotes given during her speech was a story involving Crown Prince Olaf of Norway. It would seem that the king and queen had been informally discussing the militant suffragist actions in Britain, unaware that the young prince was listening to them. Their little son interjected into the debate, asking his parents: 'Why doesn't Uncle George give women the vote?'[27]

A speech by a Miss I.S.A. Beaver concluded the meeting and was also very warmly welcomed and the general atmosphere was one of great enthusiasm. Several new members were accepted into the NUWSS, including both the mayor and Mr Brumell, and a successful collection was taken. Before the meeting broke up a resolution was carried in favour of votes for women.

***

Like so much of Emily's life, her death is shrouded in controversy and is a subject that inspires strong emotional responses. While in many ways her death can be seen in the light of a supreme sacrifice which certainly had a selfless aspect to it, there are other interpretations which cast the terrible events of that day in a rather more selfish light. Certainly, when Emily placed herself in front of King George V's horse Anmer during the Epsom Derby on 4 June 1913 she demonstrated little concern for the safety of Herbert Jones, Anmer's jockey, or for that of the other jockeys and the following horses. One of Jones's colleagues, Steve Donoghue, who was a top jockey and who was riding in the race that day said that he was lucky not to have been unseated and claimed that 'it was a miracle six more horses had not been brought down'. He was in little doubt as to Emily's actions, stating later that Emily's behaviour was 'criminal folly brought on by the freak of a mad woman's brain'.[28] This harsh assessment is understandable from a man who had just witnessed a shocking incident, had narrowly avoided being unseated and had just seen a friend and colleague injured. Indeed, the footage does clearly show at least two horses desperately trying to avoid the prone forms of Anmer, Jones and Emily.

Her reasons for this dark train of thought were numerous. Emily had suffered severely after her repeated bouts of imprisonment and force-feeding (by this point she had been arrested nine times, been on hunger strike seven times and had been force-fed on no less than forty-nine occasions). The effects of such hardships were not solely confined to the physical and must surely have had a mental impact upon Emily as well. Secondly, she had been in financial difficulties and her career was not progressing as she had wished. Her efforts at establishing herself as a journalist had met with some success, but recently there had been repeated rejections of her articles and this had undoubtedly shaken her and caused her some distress. Likewise, her efforts at poetry went unrewarded. Shortly before her death she received a terse letter from an editor who was already annoyed after being 'pestered' by Emily over an unsolicited article which he had turned down for publication, regarding her recent submission of a poem. He brutally and scathingly replied that, although the subject matter of the poem had possibilities, the poetry itself was poorly fashioned. Such a brutal appraisal would have been objectionable to any writer, but to someone in Emily's frame of mind could well have been devastating. Thirdly, and to Emily, most depressing of all was the attitude of the WSPU towards her. Emily had never been offered an official role within the organization and the higher echelons of the group looked upon Emily with some suspicion and were very wary of her. This attitude had its origins in Emily's own brand of determined and radical militancy. From being trusted when she first joined the WSPU, Emily had repeatedly taken militant actions without the approval of the hierarchy and had often refrained from even discussing her actions with the group. This radical individualism had led to mistrust on both sides and it seems clear that by 1913 Emily was viewed as something of a loose cannon. This reputation would seem to have spread, and Emily's attempts to find a secure position with other suffragist groups also met with failure and letters of rejection which must have surely further eroded her frame of mind. Emily's stubbornness and her refusal to comply with what she saw as the emptiness of some of the threats made by the WSPU had encouraged her in some of her unapproved endeavours. It was this very character that had seen Emily's paid membership of the WSPU terminated. She was, in the words of Fern Riddell, 'too uncontrollable, too radical, too inclined to seek violence without official sanction' for the hierarchy of the organization.[29]

These factors seem to have further convinced Emily that a supreme sacrifice was necessary to further the cause. This is clearly visible in her last written works in which she almost seems to have been convincing herself that not only was such a sacrifice required but that it was also worthy, even noble. One historian has convincingly described these works as being almost like a long-drawn-out suicide note. It would certainly seem that by early 1913 Emily had become even more convinced that the cause of women's suffrage required a supreme sacrifice if it was to move forward and that she herself should be the one to step forward into the breach.

Emily had always been a complicated personality, but by this stage of her life it seems clear that her obsession with the cause of women's suffrage had crossed over into what might accurately be described as fanaticism. It would appear that Emily's conversation was almost solely concerned with the struggle and this had resulted in the loss of several friends who were somewhat perturbed and, perhaps, even intimidated by the determined obsession that she showed. Emily had always been a forceful character in her own way: she had tried to organize her siblings while still a child, and this, combined with her obsessive interest in the cause, may have caused some to regard her askance. Indeed, her mother had asked her to refrain from discussing the cause of suffrage when she was staying in Longhorsley, only for Emily to still insist on insinuating the subject into her conversations.

The question of whether or not Emily intended to commit suicide on that June day has become a fierce debate with strong emotions on both sides. Trying to analyze the available evidence, the author believes that Emily was intent on making a grand gesture and was quite aware of the fact that she would likely suffer serious injury or worse, so she would have been fully aware of the dangers. She was a woman of impressive intelligence and, given her upbringing, would certainly have been familiar with horses. Even though there is little evidence of Emily being a rider herself, she had been brought up in an era when horses were commonplace. Indeed, when she was employed as a governess, the local hunt met outside her employer's home. Tens of thousands of horses were in use in London on a daily basis and horses were extensively used in the agricultural land surrounding Morpeth and Longhorsley. There have been some claims that Emily and other Northumbrian suffragettes had practised pinning flags or pennants onto the bridles of trotting horses on Morpeth Common. There is no evidence to back up this suggestion; besides which, pinning a flag to the bridle of a sedately trotting pony is a very different proposition to that of managing the same feat with a powerful racehorse galloping flat out in race conditions. Looking closely at the footage, digitized and cleaned up for a Channel 4 documentary on the hundredth anniversary of Emily's death, it seems clear that Emily did indeed identify Anmer and that she deliberately placed herself in front of the horse. If attempting to place something on the bridle, she would surely have stepped to the side, yet she made no such attempt.

Rumours abounded in the immediate aftermath of the shocking event and have continued to spread ever since. One of the conclusions of the Channel 4 documentary was that Emily did attempt to sling a flag or sash around the neck of the horse. The author remains unconvinced as the footage is still rather unclear. It was reported that this flag (actually a sash or scarf) was reputedly gathered from the course and it was subsequently put up for auction by Sotheby's and is now in the House of Commons. This item is, however, in all likelihood a forgery or fraud; indeed, Sotheby's sold it as reputedly being the flag borne by Emily, and the evidence of the seller that her father was clerk of the course on the day of the race has been proven to be false with Michael Tanner identifying him as being a London docker with no connection to racing (the actual clerk of the course was Henry Mayson Dorling). The only flags reported to have been found by the police were the two that were sewn into the back of Emily's jacket. According to horse-racing historian Michael Tanner, the two flags in Emily's possession measured 113cm x 69cm while the flag sold by Sotheby's was far larger at 210cm x 30cm. A flag of this size would definitely have been visible in the footage. In 2013, the scarf from the Houses of Parliament was displayed in Morpeth as part of the 'Emily Inspires' events, despite the fact that its true provenance is in great doubt. Indeed, while the footage of Emily does seem to show that, perhaps, she did have something in her hand, it is impossible to say what it was or even if it was simply a fault on the film.[30]

Michael Tanner concluded that Emily bringing down the king's horse was purely happenstance. He claimed that she could not have identified the horse either from markings or the jockey's colours from her position on Tattenham Corner. Subsequent evidence seems to contradict this opinion. Firstly, the restored footage clearly shows that Emily was positioned closer to the beginning of the bend than had previously been thought, and this would have enabled her to obtain a far better view of the horses and jockeys. Furthermore, the footage clearly seems to show Emily selecting the horse in front of which she positioned herself and it seems clear, at least to this author, that she deliberately intended the target of her actions to be Anmer.

As far as is known, Emily left behind no note describing her intent and it would seem, characteristically, that she had not discussed her plans in any detail with friends or family. Certainly, her family was left both shocked and baffled over her actions on that fateful day. As she lay comatose in hospital following the incident, a letter from her mother lay at her bedside. In it, Margaret communicated her sense of bewilderment over her daughter's actions and portrayed a bitterness at the perceived lack of appreciation brought about by Emily's dedication. In her letter, Margaret wrote that she could not 'believe that you could do such a dreadful act. Even for the Cause which I know you have given up your whole heart and soul to, and it has done so little in return for you.'[31]

It is known that on the night before her ill-fated trip to Epsom Emily had met with one of her closest friends within the WSPU, Kitty Marion. Emily had first met Kitty when they were imprisoned together in Newcastle in 1909. They had immediately formed a bond of strong friendship based upon the fact that they were both fiery and determined women, dedicated to the cause, and in many ways the two had 'found in each other kindred spirits'.[32] Kitty, from her very first acquaintance with Emily, had been aware of her comrade's total commitment and remarked how Emily 'had always expressed great faith in the dramatic death of a woman arousing public opinion sufficiently to compel the Government to pass the necessary franchise bill to stop further militancy'.[33]

Emily, who had become something of an embarrassment to the higher echelons of the WSPU, suddenly found favour in death which she had not secured in life. The Pankhursts, somewhat hypocritically, were especially fulsome in their praise of the fallen heroine, for this was how they had decided Emily was to be remembered. As we have already heard, suffragettes had died before as a result of force-feeding, but their sacrifices were not commemorated in anything like the same way as Emily's tragic death.

Amid all the rhetoric, the movement began plans for a hugely impressive and public funeral which was very much both a show of strength for the suffragettes but also a calculated publicity stunt designed to make a statement and to hammer home the sacrifice that Emily had made. Suffragette Grace Roe was responsible for the planning. Emily's body was moved by train to London on 14 June (a Saturday) and was met at the station by more than 3,000 women, many of them dressed in white with black armbands. Her coffin was loaded onto a waiting carriage and was drawn through the streets of London via Buckingham Palace Road. Funeral wreaths covered the bier with one such, prominently displayed, reading: 'She died for Women'.

Emily's family was probably less impressed by this publicity but went along with it at this stage. Travelling in a carriage behind the coffin were her mother Margaret, sister Letitia and one of her half-brothers, Captain Henry Davison, who was described in the press as the chief mourner. They were accompanied by a Miss Morrison who the press described tantalizingly and, perhaps, with a hint of salaciousness, as Emily's 'intimate companion'. The identity of Miss Morrison has been disputed over the years. There are three main candidates. Two belonged to the WSPU. Evelyn Mary Morrison was a noted activist who had taken part in several acts of defiance with Emily. Miss Sybil Morrison was a 20-year-old lesbian and another active member, despite her young years. The most likely candidate, however, was a local Northumbrian woman and distant relative, who had acted as a companion to Emily when she spent time recuperating in Longhorsley. This, as we have seen, was something akin to a family tradition and it seems, at least to this author, given the privacy that was shortly afterwards demanded by the Davison family, she was the most likely candidate by far. Some of Emily's extended family followed behind in two more carriages. Another carriage, conspicuously empty, was also prominent in order to draw attention to the fact that Emmeline Pankhurst had been to attend the procession but was arrested on her doorstep under the Cat and Mouse Act and imprisoned.

The carriage bearing Emily's coffin was escorted by Sylvia Pankhurst and five members of the WSPU, while eight young members of the Newcastle branch of the WSPU followed behind bearing lilies and a banner emblazoned with Joan of Arc's motto 'Fight on, God will give the Victory'. Suffragette Elsie Howey, dressed as Joan of Arc, rode upon a white horse near the front of the procession and the cross was borne by the instantly recognizable figure of Charlotte 'Charlie' Marsh. As we have heard, Newcastle-born Charlie Marsh had taken part in several actions with Emily and the two were friends.

Among the thousands who followed the procession were many who had undergone hunger strikes and a large number of the suffragettes bore banners praising Emily's sacrifice and espoused liberty and their cause. The suffragettes were welcomed by a large number of socialists who turned out at the procession to demonstrate their solidarity with the suffrage movement. Postmen, who were engaged in a strike at the time, sent wreaths to be borne in the procession, including from one depot where Davison had set a letterbox alight, while, as we have heard, large numbers of dockers also turned out in support. In a remarkable and often undocumented show of sympathy, the wife of Anmer's jockey Herbert Jones also turned up to pay her respects.

Not all were supportive, however. The non-militant NUWSS made it very clear that they did not support Emily's actions, urged their members not to attend, and even declined to send a wreath. Some suffragists went even further with, for example, the secretary of the London Society for Women's Suffrage, Philippa Strachey, writing that her group was to take no part in the funeral. She acknowledged that Emily had acted in good faith, but stated that her actions, in endangering innocent lives, would only damage the cause.

Along the route of the procession there were sporadic outbreaks of disapproval and on at least one occasion bricks were thrown at the carriage bearing the coffin. Other disapproving voices cried out 'The king's horse!' or 'Three cheers for the king's jockey!' The majority of the crowds, however, were either supportive or at least respectful, and on several occasions dissenting voices were cried down by those who were more supportive. The police maintained a close watch on the procession, focusing more upon the suffragettes taking part than on any of the dissenters.

The procession terminated at St George's Church in Bloomsbury where some 6,000 women awaited. After the service, a vigil comprising suffragettes guarded the coffin until it was moved at noon on Sunday to King's Cross.

The coffin was taken by rail north to Morpeth with the train making frequent stops so that people could pay their respects or just gawp at the coffin that it bore. Upon arrival at Morpeth Station the wreaths were unloaded; this task alone took an hour. Then the coffin was taken by carriage through the town, where an estimated 20,000 people had gathered. This was a massive turnout in the small, quiet market town and was indicative not only of fellow feeling for a Northumbrian, killed in tragic circumstances, but of the widespread support for the cause of women's suffrage that could be found in the area. As the procession moved through the streets there was no barracking, only respectful silence.

Once the procession reached the fourteenth-century church of St Mary the Virgin, the family took over responsibility for the funeral arrangements and it is clear that they wished the ceremony to be private and largely free of political statement. The arrival of the coffin was met with the Benwell Silver Band playing *La Marseillaise* and there followed a respectful service, after which Emily was laid to rest in the family plot with a gravestone erected upon which was the inscription 'Deeds not words'.

In recent years, Emily's life and sacrifice have rightly been recognized and undoubtedly she was a courageous and singularly determined woman who gave herself utterly to what was an incredibly worthy cause. There was, however, a darker side to Emily's nature and this also needs to be recognized. Like any who are fiercely dedicated to a cause – perhaps even obsessed is not too strong a word – Emily could be dismissive of any who were not as determined. Her fierce dedication resulted in her losing friends and sacrificing any chance of an otherwise normal life. Perhaps, however, the most worrying aspect of Emily's character, certainly in her last years, was an impulsive and utter disdain for the risk that her radical activities posed to the lives of others. If the planting of explosive devices at Lloyd George's partially constructed new home was Emily's work, as seems likely, this would quite likely have resulted in death if anyone had been at the property, while the devices still posed a risk to those workmen who were tasked with clearing the debris. Her attack on the unfortunate minister likewise shows a lack of concern and judgement but, of course, the greatest example of this trend in Emily's life came in her final act.

None of this detracts from Emily's cause or her determination to see that women were enfranchised, but it should be considered and acknowledged alongside the many favourable aspects of her personality. If we are to truly remember Emily, let us do so in as full a manner as we can rather than through eulogizing all the positive aspects of her cause and sacrifice while ignoring the realities of her struggle. Emily deserves that.

With war just a matter of weeks away, the support of the miners in Northumberland seemed to have remained firmly with the suffragettes. At the meeting of the Miners' Gala at Morpeth, a large meeting with representatives from all over the county, a resolution was passed calling on the government to 'at once abandon forcible feeding, to repeal the "Cat and Mouse Act", and to give to women equal voting rights with men, this session'. During the debate, the miners expressed their 'deep indignation at the torture of women by forcible feeding and the "Cat and Mouse Act"' and the resolution was passed with only one dissenter.[34] Among the many speeches given at the gala were two that largely concentrated on the issues surrounding women's suffrage and urged miners to back the cause. Members of the NUWSS were active throughout the gala, selling copies of the newspaper *Common Cause*. Their efforts met with success as it was estimated that an impressive '300 copies were disposed of'.[35]

Lydia Becker.
(by Susan Isabel Dacre, public domain)

Howick Hall,
home of Earl Grey.
(CC2.0 John Nicholson)

Fallodon Hall c.1932,
home of Viscount Grey.
(source unknown)

Miss Alison Garland, c.1922.
(Illustrated London News)

Emily Davison, pictured in Votes for Women following one of her spells in prison.

Augustine Birrell, Chief Secretary for Ireland.

Horses take avoiding action after Emily is struck by the king's horse. *(Public domain)*

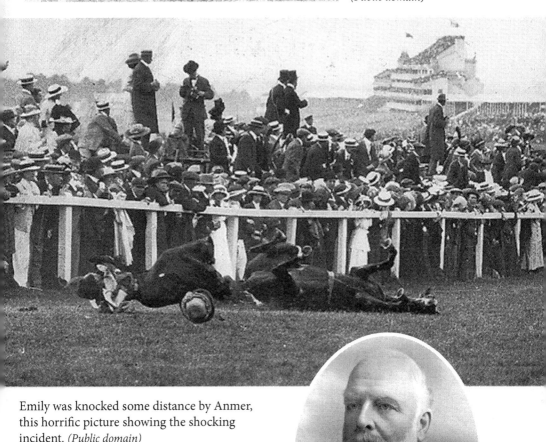

Emily was knocked some distance by Anmer, this horrific picture showing the shocking incident. *(Public domain)*

Henry Mayson Dorling in 1896, clerk of the course at Epsom. *(Public domain)*

Prison photograph of Emily's friend, the actress and radical suffragette Kitty Marion. *(Public domain)*

Front cover of The Suffragette magazine dedicated to Emily.
(© acrogame/Adobe Stock)

The funeral procession, with banner. *(Public domain)*

The carriage bearing Emily's coffin with escort. *(Public domain)*

The funeral procession in Piccadilly Circus (empty carriage visible behind). *(Illustrated London News)*

The funeral procession outside the church. *(Public domain)*

Suffragette guard of honour at King's Cross. *(Daily Mail)*

Emily's funeral procession moving towards Morpeth.
(The Journal)

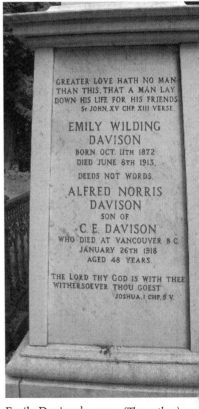

GREATER LOVE HATH NO MAN
THAN THIS, THAT A MAN LAY
DOWN HIS LIFE FOR HIS FRIENDS
St JOHN. XV CHP. XIII VERSE

EMILY WILDING
DAVISON
BORN OCT. 11th 1872
DIED JUNE 8TH 1913.

DEEDS NOT WORDS.

ALFRED NORRIS
DAVISON
SON OF
C. E. DAVISON
WHO DIED AT VANCOUVER B.C.
JANUARY 26TH 1918
AGED 48 YEARS.

THE LORD THY GOD IS WITH THEE
WITHERSOEVER THOU GOEST
JOSHUA. I CHP. 9 V.

Emily Davison's grave. *(The author)*

Dr Coxon at Malta, middle row, third from left.
(Source unknown)

Women of the Land
Army dipping sheep
at East Shaftoe.
(Daily Mirror)

The 'sex crusaders' Robert Wheatley (l) and Denise
Ingram (r). *(Daily Mirror)*

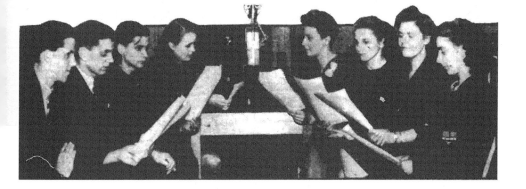

Has every available Berwick girl
volunteered yet ?

Every day is precious now if we're to beat Hitler.

Make a note of all the things you want to know about the A.T.S. . . . Then go right away and see the interviewing officer.

There are dozens of interesting jobs in the A.T.S.— one of them is yours.

Britain is calling you to come and volunteer now— ahead of your age group.

Kine-Theodolite Operator   Catering

500 girls must volunteer from BERWICK

A180562

Driver or Mechanic   Telephone or Teleprinter Operator

200,000 ATS
urgently needed

Go now and have a talk at your local employment exchange or A.T.S. or Army Recruiting Centre.

Full details at the Employment Exchange in Scott's Place, Castlegate, Berwick.

Recruitment advert for the ATS.
(Berwick Advertiser)

Mary, Princess Royal and Countess of Harewood in 1926. *(Public domain)*

Corporal Anne Falla. *(Berwickshire News)*

CHAPTER THREE

The First World War

The majority of the women of Northumberland, no matter what their stance on suffrage, threw their support behind the war effort and undertook whatever measures they thought they could to assist. For many this involved voluntary work and fund-raising, while others decided to use their skills in first-aid (or to learn those skills) and organization to help. Recognizing that the war would no doubt be a bloody affair, the Alnwick detachments of the Red Cross, for example, quickly swung into action, spurred on by the enthusiasm of their two commandants, Lady Victoria Percy and Mrs G. Leather-Culley. It was quickly agreed that the local National Schools would be used as a base hospital and that other locations could be acquired as necessary.

The week before the bank holiday during which war became inevitable had seen the Morpeth detachment of the Red Cross in a training camp at Longhirst Hall and as the crisis in Europe deepened they were put on alert to be ready for service at twelve hours' notice.[1] In common with other towns across Northumberland, buildings had been requisitioned for use as military hospitals. In Morpeth, the Red Cross, under the local leadership of the Honourable Mrs Joicey of Longhirst Hall, took over control of the former Borough School, which had been equipped to operate as a hospital.[2] Mrs Joicey made an appeal on behalf of the hospital at the Borough Hall, which was now being equipped and brought to a war footing, in which she asked for donations of money from the people of Morpeth, adding that no amount was too small. Despite the assurance that the hospital was being rapidly equipped, a further appeal for numerous items seems to show that much vital equipment was lacking. Mrs Joicey also asked for small tables, sheets, pillow cases, blankets, nightshirts, bed-jackets, men's slippers, hot water bottles and covers, bed socks, mackintoshes, old linen, tea towels, towels, dish cloths, dusters, brushes, combs and hairbrushes, sponges, soap, sewing materials, candlesticks and candles.[3]

With mass recruitment, and Alnwick being selected as a training base, it was obvious that large numbers of soldiers, the majority of whom would be strangers to the area, would soon be present in the town. The townspeople formed a committee to provide suitable entertainment for these men and, alongside it, a women's committee consisting of Mrs Mangin, Miss Turnbull of Bailiffgate, Mrs Reavely, Mrs T.S. Kyle and Miss Kate Douglas was also formed and performed good work throughout the war.

As the first wartime Christmas approached there was much consideration given as to how the season should be celebrated when so many men were in danger at the front. Some advocated its cancellation, but wiser heads realized that the season provided a welcome relief from the stresses of living in wartime Britain and the majority of Alnwick people managed to have some form of traditional celebration despite the raised prices. For many Northumbrian women, the prospect of celebrating Christmas was dampened by the spectre of missing loved ones and by increased prices, but most remained determined to get on with things as normally as possible. Many female members of the local aristocracy viewed it as their duty to ensure that the less well off could enjoy as pleasant a Christmas as possible. The inmates of Alnwick Workhouse, for example, were treated to a Christmas lunch and gifts. The gifts were distributed on behalf of the guardians, but also by Lady Victoria Percy who visited the inmates over the Christmas period.

The voluntary efforts of local women continued to contribute to the war effort throughout 1915 and, as the year ended, the womenfolk of Alnwick remained keen to do as much as possible. On Saturday, 11 December the Duchess's School held a sale at the Assembly Rooms to raise money for the War Loan Fund.

The day began with the awarding of school prizes by Lady Victoria Percy (who also distributed Cambridge Local and music certificates which had been earned). Included among the prizes was the special prize for head girl and a games brooch to Evelyn Temperley, a form work and Senior Cambridge Honours prize to E. Pentleton, and a scripture prize and Senior Cambridge Certificate to J. Purvis. The Reverend Canon Mangin, vicar of Alnwick, then pronounced the sale open, with stalls selling a wide variety of goods. Through such voluntary efforts, both large and small, the women of Northumberland made an active and very welcome contribution to the national effort, both at home and on the various fighting fronts.

Although much attention was lavished on the army, the people of Morpeth made sure to remember the activities and sacrifices of the men of the Royal Navy and in July a branch depot was set up at the Butter Market to collect fresh garden produce for distribution to the North Sea Fleet.[4] The centre was to be open every Wednesday (market day) from 9.00 am until noon and Morpeth residents were urged to give generously with all gifts gratefully received. The centre had been the brainchild of Mrs Ralph Spencer and Mrs Fenwick and within the space of a week the response from farmers and townspeople had been great. There were donations not only of produce but also of money to purchase vegetables and fruit, and nine large crates were dispatched to the fleet on Wednesday, 14 July with more to follow.

Saturday, 6 March 1915 had seen the annual hiring fair for the employment of agricultural workers take place in Alnwick Corn Market. There were reported to be a large number of both farmers and those seeking employment present, and demand for labour was high due to the numbers of men who had allegedly left to join up. As a result of this, the wages for workers also increased notably. Estimates put the average increase at between 1s and 2s per week, making the weekly average 19s to 23s along with the usual benefits of free housing, 1,000 yards of potatoes planted, coal supply and, in many cases, a small garden. Wages for women had also increased to an average of 12s per week along with 3s per day for twenty days of harvesting. Given the supposed shortage of manpower, youths were also hired in large numbers with wages being based on age and experience, ranging from 8s to 15s per week.

The shortages of labour grew worse as the year continued and by the time of the half-annual hirings in November there was a dearth of males available for engagement. As a result of this, the market for women, young men and lads was far more competitive than normal. Because of this the wages became greatly inflated and 'Where young lads were engaged it was at large increase of wages.'[5] The wages demanded by and granted to females were also inflated by the shortages.

Table 1) Agricultural Wages (half-yearly) in November 1915

Category	Wages (half-yearly)
Girls	£3 10s to £6
Young Women	£8 and £9 to £13
Lads	£10 to £12
Young Men	£12 and £16 to £19

The half-annual hirings held in Morpeth also resulted in a poor turnout, but the number of girls and young women was said to be high with a brisk trade at higher wages than average. As could be expected, the numbers of lads and young men was very depressed, but those who were present were taken on at a substantial increase in wages.

With the growing problem of the lack of able-bodied men to undertake physical work, attitudes of many Morpethians towards women in the workforce were undergoing a radical shift. Roles involving hard manual labour, often in dirty conditions, had previously been seen as unsuitable for women (the exception being agricultural work), but by mid-December it was clear that women would be able, indeed would be expected, to undertake such roles. The town council ordered the surveyor to compile a list of those women who would be willing to undertake duties in cleaning the roads. The women who were appointed would be paid at a rate of 6d per hour.

The shortages of available agricultural labour continued throughout the war and this led to many female farm labourers becoming used to the twin benefits of better wages and living conditions combined with more bargaining power to further better their conditions. In 1916, the March hirings were severely affected by a dearth of young male workers as so many had joined up, many of whom were to be killed just months later on the Somme. The hirings were further affected by the fact that, because of the shortages of men, those servants, male and female, who were present knew that farmers were desperate and that they could, as a result, demand higher advances on their wages. The majority of farmers were left with little choice but to acquiesce to these demands. Men with accompanying women workers, a throwback to the bondager method of working, were thus hired at a weekly rate of 26s to 28s, along with benefits listed on p61. Women were generally afforded the rate of 13s to 15s with an advance of twenty days for the harvest period and youngsters under the age of military service could demand 10s to 15s according to their agricultural experience. Many servants remained in their current positions (there was little flitting), but were confident of demanding increased rates of an extra 4s to 5s per week.

This continued throughout the year, with the November hirings proving to be particularly problematic as the number of single servants was very low and many chose to remain with their current employers (although again at an increased rate) and those who did find alternative employment contracts did so at an inflated wage. For other women, the opportunity of high wages and perceived freedom from agricultural labour, with its tied property and so on, tempted them away to the factories which were increasingly coming to rely upon female labour to fulfil wartime orders, and many a Northumbrian woman left rural Northumberland to undertake munitions or other industrial work, either on Tyneside or further afield.

Nationally, the government believed that women could be the salvation of the agricultural labour crisis and efforts were made to ascertain how effective women might be in farming and how they might be recruited and trained. This provoked a rather tetchy and ambivalent letter to the *Morpeth Herald* in April. The writer claimed that nowhere near enough attention was given to the vast amount of farm work already being undertaken by women in northern England and Scotland and claimed that instead of going to France to assess the effectiveness of women farm workers, the government should have looked closer to home. However, the writer claimed that women who were not used to such work were unlikely to be of much use as they lacked the necessary physical and mental aptitudes and, in many cases, were frightened of livestock. He also pointed out that much farm work was seasonal and weather-dependent and that women were of no use in cold weather as they could not be sent out to do odd jobs in such conditions. Clearly some Morpethian men remained unconvinced of the determination, toughness and abilities of some non-country-born women.

Not everyone shared these concerns and the lord lieutenant of Northumberland announced the formation of the Northumberland Guild of War Agricultural Helpers which would act as an organizer of casual labour and as an agent for those women who found more permanent work on specific farms. The guild would have district officers who would look after the interests of their members under the guidance of the head warden, Mrs Straker of Hexham. One of the districts was centred on Morpeth and substantial numbers of women quickly began submitting their names to the guild.

One area in which women faced absolute opposition was in their possible employment in the mining industry. Although some women argued that this ought to be considered, the mining organizations, both unions and owners, were categorically against this development. They claimed that such work would lead to a decline in both the physical and moral development of women, who were not suited to such labour. The local miners argued that it would be far more suitable to allow former miners to return to the work instead of inflicting the work upon women.

Many Morpeth women were lured away from housekeeping or, increasingly, domestic service by the wages and opportunities of working within the munitions industries and a large number of Morpeth women found work in the factories of Tyneside such as the Elswick Works of Armstrong's; others replaced men who had worked at the local iron foundry, Swinney's. The work they undertook was dirty, strenuous and very dangerous, with many women being injured or killed while working in these industries.

The attitudes towards women workers continued to be ambivalent among many sections of Northumbrian society and some businessmen showed a marked distrust of female employees and a deep unwillingness to employ them, regardless of the national situation. In 1916, for example, the compulsory call-up of a man employed by a Morpeth shoe shop, R. Rutherford & Sons, was opposed by the man's employer who asked for him to be excused but was told to find an older man to do his work. They claimed at tribunal that they could not do so, and that it was impossible for women to undertake his work. The employers were reluctant to release Mr Bailey to attend the hearing, and upon learning that his main duties were the packing of boots, for which women certainly were qualified, the military representative commented that it seemed that the firm simply did not want to be inconvenienced and the appeal was dismissed.

While the increased wages available to many women were of benefit, there were some who had little hope of furthering themselves and, for many, living conditions continued to be appalling. A case in 1916 at Morpeth highlighted the extremely poor living conditions endured by some. Mrs Sarah Cook was brought before the bench charged with desertion of her five children. Mr Cook was in the army but was a deserter who had not been traced, while their eldest son had just been sent to an industrial school. Mrs Cook had continued to claim her army allowance despite her husband being an absentee and had been under active police surveillance. She had deserted her children for almost a week and had previously pawned her eldest child's boots. It was claimed that the family home was in a 'wretched state' with practically 'nothing to eat ... in the house, and nothing to cover the children when they went to bed'. Mrs Cook was remanded, while her long-suffering children were sent to the Morpeth workhouse.

By 1917, the shortage of available men for the workforce was acute and women were increasingly being welcomed into new roles. As Northumberland was largely an agricultural county, it was no surprise that many of the local women volunteered to be trained in agricultural work, seeing the increased wages as a particular benefit. In April, an appeal went out asking for 10,000 women to come forward for duties in agriculture. Half would be trained in milking and dairy work, while the other half would be trained in general farm work. The director general of National Service assured women that there would be no delay in getting them onto the farms and working as it was vital that food supplies were maintained. He went on to say that successful volunteers would, within ten days, be sent to a farm with a free railway pass, free training and a month's maintenance payment.

The new opportunities and increased wages on offer to many women had a concomitant effect on lower paid and less popular jobs, especially those in service. With the growing numbers of women applying for jobs in either the munitions industries or in agriculture, the better-off in Morpeth were faced with a shortage of available house and farm servants. The numbers of situations vacant adverts throughout the year highlight this. One page in August included adverts for a kitchen girl who was able to milk for Mrs W.S. Sanderson of Northgate, Morpeth; a general servant who was able to cook and bake for Mrs R.N. Swinney of Morpeth and Newbiggin-by-the-Sea; and a cook-general (no washing), to work at the Kirkhill, Cambo property of Mrs Adamson (who preferred a country woman for the post). Interestingly the same page also contained an advert from a young woman who was seeking employment and was eager to begin a career in office work.

The lack of servants saw a concomitant effect on the agencies which found employment for such men and women. In Morpeth one of the main agencies was Mrs Dobson's (formerly the late Mr Purdy's) of 67 Newgate Street, Morpeth. In August, the agency was advertising for cooks and general servants who had good references and, demonstrating the staff shortages, offering good rates of pay. Other vacancies advertised by Dobson's included an urgent demand for several maids to work at farmhouses. These maids would be expected to undertake some milking and, indicating a mistrust of the reliability of young women who might seek more highly paid positions, the adverts said that elderly women would be preferred.

Women, as we have seen, were also key in many fund-raising ventures during the war. A series of women's days were held in Morpeth in September and October which demonstrated how effective such small ventures could be by raising the total of £105 10s for a number of wartime causes. The days were organized by a committee chaired by the mayoress and included entertainments, and stalls selling a wide variety of items.

The shortage of agricultural workers continued right up until and beyond the end of the war. In the final year of the war the hirings once more reflected the increased shortages of skilled labour within Northumberland, and in March there were said to be thin pickings with men being able to request weekly wages of 35s to 38s and some with particular skills or experience earning up to 42s; women were able to demand 18s per week and an increase of a few shillings per day over twenty days of harvest.

An address by Mrs Renwick to a crowd at Morpeth in 1918 demonstrated that traditional viewpoints towards women had not entirely changed as a result of the war and that the maternalistic (and patronizing) view of the upper classes towards the lower classes had not changed. Mrs Renwick stated that a woman's first duty was to her home and to ensure that it was as welcoming as possible for her menfolk when they returned, and that it was women who had fewer responsibilities and who should therefore seek work away from the home. Mrs Renwick 'impressed upon the women of Morpeth to be ready for their sons and husbands when they came back ... and make their homes bright and cheerful: that was the great work which women had to do who were not in uniform'.[6]

By the summer of 1918 the local miners' attitudes towards women workers had softened somewhat, however, with the Northumberland Miners' Association and the Coal Owners' Association having agreed that, given the extreme shortages of manpower, it would be acceptable to allow women to work on the surface in specific duties ranging from working in colliery shops to timber yards.

Even at this late stage in the war, women were urged to consider joining the various nursing services that were caring for injured soldiers at the front. A recruitment meeting for the Queen Mary's Army Auxiliary Corps (who sent women to the Western Front and other locations to act as drivers, clerks, waitresses, cooks, etc.) was held in Morpeth during the summer of 1918. A contingent of the corps from Gateshead, led by a Miss Guest, arrived at the railway station and was met by the pipe band which escorted them to the Market Place. A large crowd assembled and, after the presentation to Robert Clark, the women of the QMAAC were welcomed to the district. The mayor stated that he hoped local women would come forward and give their names to the ladies of the corps who were present. The members of the QMAAC, led by the pipe band, then paraded through the main streets of Morpeth attracting a large and interested crowd before they assembled at the YMCA rooms for tea. Following tea, the recruitment meeting was held in the evening at the YMCA Hall with a lecture and programme of musical entertainment. The lecture, given by Miss Hingston, was an urgent appeal for new recruits who, she said, would make a real difference to the men fighting the war. Miss Hingston had originally served in the VAD (Voluntary Aid Detachment) in France before transferring to the Women's Army Auxiliary Corps (now renamed the QMAAC). She was thus able to give a stirring account of the activities of these women's groups at the front. The corps was particularly looking for young women who could act as typists, clerks, cooks and waitresses, but Miss

Hingston reiterated that the activities of members of the corps were diverse and interesting. After thanking the mayor, the pipe band and the Boy Scouts (who had accompanied the parade) moved once more to the Market Place where a night recruitment meeting was held. Once again there were speeches, this time from Company Sergeant Major Carmichael who had also served abroad with the QMAAC. She said that she hoped many of those present would come forward, and once again said that 'any girl who joined the corps would never regret it. The life was a happy one.' Perhaps attempting to soothe worried parents, she stated that 'the welfare of the girls was never lost sight of.'[7] Afterwards the women were escorted by the pipe band back to the station.

Despite the earlier evidence of women being increasingly willing to break the law when necessary, many men continued to harbour outdated attitudes towards the opposite sex, and magistrates tended to judge women brought before them very firmly indeed during the war, even for very minor offences. In February 1915, for example, two married women from Alnwick were convicted of using language unfit for repetition. PC Robson had overheard the two (Rachel Drummond of Stamp's Yard and Isabella Lundy of Union Court) arguing in Union Court and was disgusted by the 'extremely filthy language' they were using.[8] Upon presenting his case, PC Robson wrote down the terms of abuse used and showed them to the bench (but of course would not repeat them). The chairman, Major S.F. Widdrington, declared that such cases were on the increase and that the language used was disgraceful. The authorities were determined to stamp out such behaviour and the two were fined the sum of 20s apiece.

Despite the ongoing war there were still domestic concerns and one of these even involved a long and arduous trip to give advice to an ally for one female Alnwick doctor. Dr Beatrice Coxon had been born in Oldham and had qualified from Edinburgh School of Medicine for Women in 1909 and by the following year was the house surgeon at Alnwick Infirmary and a member of the North of England branch of the British

Medical Association. In April 1915 she, along with several female colleagues, had journeyed to Serbia where she served in a tented hospital run by Mrs St Clair Stobart. She later served in a similar capacity in Salonika before the hospital was evacuated as the Germans overran the country.

In January 1916, Dr Coxon was dispatched to Russia along with two female colleagues to give advice on women's health at the request of the tsarina. Her mission changed and she found herself in charge of the British Women's Maternity Unit for Russia which had been organized and sponsored by the NUWSS. The trip, during wartime and with the dangers of severe winter weather, would have been particularly hazardous and no doubt this was exacerbated by the febrile political climate in Russia at the time.

A month later, the authorities asked women who were registered as doctors if they would be willing to submit their names for service with the Royal Army Medical Corps. Almost fifty women did so and Dr Coxon was among the first. Despite this seeming change of procedures, the women in fact found themselves employed as civilian contractors on twelve-month contracts to the RAMC with a salary of 24s per day and a promised gratuity of £60 at the end of service. Her wartime service saw Dr Coxon posted to the Tigne Military Hospital at Malta where she served for a year before returning to Britain.

With many medical facilities and professionals being preoccupied with military casualties, there had been concerns throughout the war about ways in which to provide civilians with adequate treatment. A constant concern, especially among women's groups, was the child mortality rates and the education of new mothers. Although Alnwick had lower child mortality rates than many other northern towns, there were still problems. As a result of these concerns, Alnwick Council had taken the decision to set up a maternity and child welfare centre which would offer advice and some medical services to mothers and children. Once again, the initiative was largely the idea of local women and was organized by them. The centre was governed by a committee which consisted of Lady Victoria Percy, Mrs R.R.

Mangin (who was convener), Mrs Leather-Culley (treasurer), Mrs Adam Robinson, Mrs C. Turnbull, Mrs William Bell, Mrs R. Henderson, Mrs E. Carr, Mrs F.G. Skelly and Mrs Norman Brown. Many of these committee members had made substantial donations and useful contributions of machinery, with the Duke of Northumberland purchasing a baby-weighing machine for the centre. The committee reported that in the first few weeks attendance at the centre had been very encouraging and they were hopeful that it would prove a great success.

The Red Cross also held frequent 'Our Day' appeals in Alnwick, with events in both October and early November which attracted great patronage. The event in October 1917, for example, raised the sum of £89 10s, and a further donation of £7 4s raised at a cinema entertainment given by Mr J.H. Sanderson at the Corn Exchange brought the total up to £96 14s. The November event was even more impressive and successfully raised the sum of £150. The society and the council paid tribute to those women who had organized the day and in particular to the work of Mrs Leather-Culley who had been key to its success.

As we have seen, most women in the county supported the war effort, no matter how fearfully. The authorities saw this as an opportunity for women to use their influence on young men to further encourage recruitment and in many communities young women were urged to encourage their men to volunteer for service. In early September 1914 an open-air meeting was held in Morpeth Market Square at which the mayor, Councillor Sanderson, urged every able-bodied Morpethian to volunteer and urged the women to encourage their men, saying 'To you bonnie girls who have sweethearts, don't give them the glad eye until they go and "take the bob".'[9]

Mayor Sanderson's appeal to Morpethian women to do their bit for the war effort was in effect building on a theme that had been common in the town since the beginning of the war. To some Morpethians it became obvious very quickly that women might be expected to undertake more roles within the workforce during the war and perhaps after it. Towards the end of August a short article had appeared in the local newspaper which advised that accounting might be a suitable and fairly well-paid job for educated Morpeth women, and explained that the conditions of work were congenial and pleasant and that, although some money was required for training, the best way to gain entry into this profession was to become an articled apprentice to a practising accountant and that positions were available in and around Morpeth.

Given the labour shortages and the pre-war determination of women to be considered more equally within society (and with many in Morpeth having the inspiration of the memory of Emily Davison spurring them on) it was inevitable that the women of Morpeth were anxious to become more involved and to undertake work which would, in peacetime, have been denied to them. The year 1914 saw widespread appeals both locally and nationally for women to become more involved both in the war effort and in other professional fields which would release men for front-line service.

The women from the professional classes in Morpeth were quick to organize themselves and to attempt to give perhaps slightly patronizing advice to Morpethian women on what would be expected of them during the war. In November, a meeting for women only was organized at the town hall, chaired by the wife of Dr A. Brumell, which would be addressed by a guest speaker from Newcastle. Perhaps hinting at the classes of women that the meeting was aiming to reach, the notice was at pains to make clear that there would be no collection at the meeting.

Many Northumbrian families suffered the loss of multiple male family members, and the burdens that fell upon the remaining women were very heavy indeed with limited pensions and a bleak future facing many of the women who found themselves bereft. Mrs Thomasine Blyth Egdell, a widow living at Pottergate New Row, Alnwick, had five sons who were serving; sadly for Mrs Egdell, of her five sons who were serving, four were killed during the war.

The conflict left an indelible impression upon the women of Northumberland. Many had suffered the loss of loved ones, while others were faced with the prospect of menfolk returning home too maimed to work. Still others had had their eyes opened to new possibilities, both within the fields of employment and in a wider social sense. For many of these younger women who had experienced such opportunities, the prospect of a return to the limited options of pre-war Britain was unconscionable. In many this brought about a fervent recollection of the suffragist campaign and women were increasingly demanding more of a say in how the country was run.

In 1918, the British government passed an Act granting the vote to women over the age of 30 who were householders, the wives of householders, occupiers of property with an annual rent of £5 and graduates of British universities. This gave the vote to more than 8 million women, but still left a substantial number unrepresented. However, the fears of many politicians over granting women's suffrage went unfulfilled and ten years later the vote was given to women over the age of 21 on the same basis as men.

CHAPTER FOUR

The Second World War

Faced with the probability of a second European war, the women of Britain realized that they would, once more, be expected to play a major role in the war effort. Many in Northumberland had experienced great hardship during the depression-haunted years of the inter-war period and many of the possibilities in the fields of employment that had seemed to promise so much at the end of the First World War had not come to fruition, with the majority of women reverting back to roles that would have been at least familiar to those of previous generations.

One of the greatest fears for many women was the prospect of aerial bombardment which had been seen in recent conflicts. It was clear that the families of Britain would be on the front lines of this conflict and that women would have to play a substantial role in safeguarding the population and in maintaining both morale and as normal a mode of living as was possible.

With mass evacuation from the cities and other vulnerable areas, many women in rural Northumberland found themselves being expected to take in evacuees who had little or no idea of conditions in the countryside and who were often bewildered and upset at being separated from their families. The organization of the reception committees for these evacuees almost overwhelmingly fell upon the local women of the Women's Voluntary Service (WVS) who provided not only a welcome but also food and drinks, organized billets and generally helped evacuees to settle into their new surroundings. Other women played a not inconsiderable role. In Alnwick, for example, any cases of illness among incoming evacuees were treated by a first-aid party, led by Mrs Collingwood Thorp, which had set up its base in the general waiting room of Alnwick Station; the majority of the wartime efforts on the home front depended upon the actions of volunteers such as Mrs Thorp and her party. Mrs Thorp, a member of the British Red Cross, had also been instrumental in the setting up of a first-aid post at the Northumberland Hall.

Many of the rural communities of Northumberland attempted to maintain a semblance of normality in the build-up to the war by continuing to hold their annual agricultural shows. Just the week before the war began, one of the most popular North Northumberland shows was held. Glendale Show was (and continues to be) extremely popular and a feature in the rural calendar of Northumberland. Held at Wooler, the show attracted a crowd of thousands and was described as, in the circumstances, 'a distinct triumph'.[1] All classes were described as being of a very high quality, with the best sheep and horses from both sides of the border on display. Highlighting the situation, however, was the presence of a stand representing the Women's Land Army, which was offering advice and actively recruiting under the leadership of Mrs J.G.G. Rea of Berrington. The attitude of many Northumbrian farmers, heavily influenced by their experiences during the previous war and by the fact that female farm workers had been a main fixture of Northumbrian farming until comparatively recently, was that women could, and would have to, make a vital contribution to the industry during the war. The Women's Land Army was one of the most prominent organizations in rural Northumberland at this time of crisis and across the area local group leaders were being selected: for example, Mrs Weeks of Thirston House was appointed as local recruiting officer for the Felton area and advertised that she was available to give particulars to any interested parties.

The attitude towards women working on the land was not something that fostered enthusiasm among everyone. Local organization sometimes took longer and feelings about these new agricultural workers were mixed, with many rural organizations being distrustful of what they viewed as unqualified interlopers. Indeed, the National Union of Agricultural Workers reacted to the new organization with unconcealed venom, saying in its magazine:

> The Hon. Mrs This, Lady That and the Countess of Something Else are all on the warpath again. The Women's Land Army is here, and they have all got their old jobs back – of bossing people, and of seeing that the farmers find a way out of their labour shortage without having to pay better wages.[2]

This attitude displays the class resentment that was commonplace among rural communities and the distrust that existed between the farm workers and their employers. However, it is important to point out that this was not a view held by all in Northumberland and that although distrust of the landed classes did indeed run deep within many rural Northumbrian communities, the county had a long history of employing female labour on farms and, by and large, the new volunteers were often more warmly welcomed in the county than elsewhere.[3]

There was no shortage of volunteers coming forward and the biggest problem throughout 1940 remained in how to house the young women. Many of the farms and cottages within the county were considered unsuitable, but in the Wooler district the WLA and the Young Women's Christian Association (YWCA) co-operated to begin a system of hostels that could house the women.

Using already established and respected members of the local farming community helped the WLA in Northumberland. For example, the appointment of Mr W. Smith of Ryebank, Wooler helped to ensure that the local branch of the WLA was well organized and had, at its head, someone who was respected by many local farmers. Mr Smith quickly found a suitable hostel for the current volunteers that was large enough to cope with the expected influx of newcomers, by taking over a property at Haugh Head in Wooler.

The chairman of the Northumberland War Ag (Agriculture), Major J.G.G. Rea, was keen to highlight the contribution already being made by the WLA in the county. As early as April he was able to address a meeting stating that the WLA 'had done much to relieve the shortage [of labour] ... and some of them had done very good work, even although many of them had never worked before'. Another local landowner, Rotarian J.W. Carmichael JP, demonstrated the ambiguity of feeling over the work of the WLA in his reply when he criticized the training period allotted to the young women, saying that four weeks was nowhere near enough time to train them adequately and that, indeed, the training of an 'expert in the industry' took years. Carmichael was somewhat missing the point as it was never intended that the young volunteers of the WLA would be experts in agriculture. He was, however, forced to admit that 'the work done by the WLA had been very valuable and he commended the proposed hostel scheme'.[4]

We have already seen how one of the biggest problems facing the WLA was finding suitable accommodation for the young volunteers. By April a second hostel at Pawston had been added to the one at Haugh Head in Wooler. While the Haugh Head hostel was solely run by the WLA (indeed it was the first to be so run), the new one was run by the YWCA. At both hostels wardens were employed to care for the young women (no doubt also to monitor their behaviour), and to make their surroundings as pleasant as possible. Motor transport was hired to take the women to their places of work on a daily basis.

Attitudes towards the volunteers of the WLA had also softened, with most farmers now being appreciative of the efforts of the women. In April, *Farmer and Stockbreeder* commented that the WLA was

> an indispensable feature of the war effort. Whatever may be said of women's capacity, no one will deny their zeal and willingness.... They [women] are not capable of all farm work, but the discerning farmer can find use for their services and find these services useful when well directed.[5]

By 1942 even the most reluctant farmers had to admit that the women of the Land Army were now proving their value to agriculture in Northumberland with most farmers now willing to take advantage of this additional form of labour. The women undertook almost every role on the farm, including strenuous activities such as harvesting, and shearing and dipping sheep. Without their contribution it is certain that output in Northumberland would have decreased as more men left for the armed services. At East Shaftoe several of the women were photographed and interviewed by reporters from the *Daily Mirror*. The women were hard at work in the arduous task of dipping sheep. Before the war, two of the women had been cooks.

In the spring of 1942 it became clear that the number of men who had joined up and had formerly been employed in felling timber was resulting in a slump in the availability of this precious wartime resource. Thus the government announced the formation of the Women's Timber Corps (WTC) whose volunteers quickly became known as 'Timber Jills'. The WTC would work in forestry and in sawmills and were told in advance that the work would be arduous and dirty. Despite this, volunteers came forward in numbers and the WTC was placed under the command of the WLA (of which it was officially a part). Members faced a six-week training period before being posted to a billet and undertaking their duties (which included felling, loading, driving tractors, working with horses and operating sawmills among other things); for undertaking this extremely heavy work the women were paid between 35s and 46s per week (although deductions for food, etc. reduced this significantly).

The problems faced by some Northumbrian women living in rural settings at a time when mental health issues were not well recognized or understood and where one's personal business could quickly become public knowledge sometimes resulted in tragedy. There was one such tragedy in Rothbury at the beginning of the war. A coroner's inquest into the sudden death by arsenic poisoning of Mrs Phyllis Evelyn Bell of Front Street, Rothbury, recorded the 'most extraordinary nature' of the case.[6] It would seem that poor Mrs Bell had for many years been suffering silently from severe neurosis and a variety of other nervous complaints which were resulting in severe headaches and spells of sickness. Despite the pleas of her husband, Mrs Bell had only reluctantly sought the advice of Dr Armstrong who had established that Mrs Bell's health issues were a result of her nervous anxieties. The doctor was also aware that Mrs Bell was in the habit of anonymously writing ludicrous letters to various Rothbury folk and the fact that this had become public knowledge was adding to her anxieties. Mr Bell had returned from work, as a grocer, at around 2.00 pm and had discovered his wife dead on the floor. Dr Armstrong testified that he had arranged an appointment with a nerve specialist for Mrs Bell but that she had died before this could be attended. The post-mortem showed that Mrs Bell had ingested enough arsenic to kill fifteen adults. The police were concerned as they had not been able to trace the source of the arsenic. The coroner, despite evidence pointing to suicide, was unable to reach a firm verdict and could only deliver a verdict on the cause of death as it could not be ascertained whether Mrs Bell had ingested the liquid deliberately or by accident.

Throughout the war, the authorities in Northumberland were particularly concerned by incidents of crime involving women and it is undoubtedly true that the strain of trying to maintain a home could sometimes lead to transgressions while, particularly among the younger population, the temptations offered in wartime Britain, combined with the often febrile atmosphere, could tempt them into illegal activities.

Other wartime crimes, however, were of the sort that would have no doubt occurred regardless of the national situation. In April 1941, for example, a serious case of wounding came before the bench at Rothbury. The 50-year-old Miss Isobel Jane Selby Dixon of Gate Cottage, Garleigh Road, Rothbury was accused of wounding her long-time friend Miss Jane Anne Soulsby (75) at Central Buildings, Rothbury on the night of 22 March. It would seem that the trouble between the two friends (Miss Dixon visited Miss Soulsby on an almost daily basis) had begun at the start of the year when Miss Soulsby noticed that some money had gone missing from her house at a time when Miss Dixon was her only visitor. She had asked Dixon about it, but she had denied any knowledge of the money and Soulsby later mentioned this matter to the relieving officer. On the night of Saturday, 22 March, there was a knock on Miss Soulsby's door and, upon answering, the defendant had entered the property and sat down with her hand in her coat pocket. The police officer giving evidence stated that Miss Soulsby was an elderly woman but was of sound mind and that her memory was reliable. It was alleged that Miss Dixon then accused her former friend of telling the relieving officer that she had taken money from her. She stood up, produced a bottle from her pocket, and began striking Miss Soulsby on the head so ferociously that the bottle broke and Miss Soulsby fell to the floor bleeding from head wounds. It would appear that at that point Dixon fled and after some time Soulsby managed to rouse herself and wash the blood off as best she could before alerting a neighbour who fetched a doctor and the police. After treatment, the police ascertained the story from Soulsby and spoke to Dixon who claimed that she had never left the house that night.

Giving evidence, Miss Soulsby confirmed that the two had been friends for a long time and that Dixon frequently came over to the house for her tea or supper (Miss Soulsby concluded that she had perhaps been 'too good' to Miss Dixon), but that at the start of the year she had left the defendant alone in her house peeling potatoes while she went on a message for half an hour. Later that night Miss Soulsby had noticed that £17 had gone missing. Miss Soulsby said this was 'a big loss for me' and she had asked Miss Dixon about the money several times, but the defendant had always denied any knowledge of the matter. Miss Soulsby claimed that on the night of the attack she had been about to go to bed when she went to the door and Miss Dixon walked in. She stated: 'I said I was sorry I had no supper for her. She asked if I had seen the relieving officer. Then she was into my head with the bottle, and I thought I was a gonner [*sic*]. Another blow would have finished me.' Miss Soulsby claimed she did not know how many times she was struck but that she fell to the ground and that Dixon had 'walked out, never looking behind or speaking. I said "Oh Selby Dixon".'

Miss Soulsby claimed that she had worked on cleaning her wounds all night without sleeping until 8.00 am the next day when she alerted her neighbour and asked her to get a nurse and doctor. Under cross-examination Miss Soulsby testified that the accused knew that she had the £17 (which she had saved from selling teas at the Jubilee Hall before the war) and she had 'been poaching about'. She also confirmed that despite poor eyesight she was certain in her identification of the accused. Several neighbours testified that they had seen Miss Dixon visiting regularly, with an upstairs neighbour reporting that she had heard the sound of a thump, like someone falling, at the time. Another, Miss Jane Parsons, said that when summoned by Miss Soulsby on the Sunday morning she found the latter in a 'terrible state ... her clothing ... saturated with blood' but clear-headed and that she had sent for medical attention before summoning the police at the urging of the doctor.

Given that the defendant had claimed not to have left her house on the night in question, the testimony of local bus driver George Edward Diery was particularly damning. Mr Diery, of Wagtail Road, stated that he had known both women for many years and that on the night in question he had been crossing the bridge into the village when he noticed Miss Dixon walking towards him from Bridge Street and that she had crossed the road to avoid him, but when he looked back she had crossed back again.

Dr A.S. Hedley testified that he had been summoned to attend to Miss Soulsby and found her remarkably clear-headed with little sign of concussion (although this was more than twelve hours after the attack) and upon examination he found two lacerations on her scalp. She also complained of pain in her jaw. The doctor stated it was very clear that Miss Soulsby had lost a lot of blood.

Superintendent Cruikshank stated that he had observed the broken and bloodstained bottle (which he produced as evidence) at the property of Miss Soulsby and that he had visited Miss Dixon who had denied the assault and claimed to have not left the house after 7.30 pm on the night in question. The officer arrested her and took her to the police station where he noticed that the gloves she wore bore a noticeable stain; the police sent the gloves to be analyzed at the Home Office Laboratory which concluded that there were two stains and both were human blood.

Giving her evidence, the defendant claimed that Miss Soulsby had accused her of taking $2 (she sometimes had Canadian money sent to her by a relative) and that she had said she 'would have to see about that, because she could not have Miss Soulsby spoiling her good character'.[7] She also repeated her claim to have not left her house and claimed that two ladies known to her had visited and left at around dusk, after which she went to bed. Miss Dixon claimed to have been working in her garden and said the blood on her gloves was a result of cutting herself on a gooseberry bush. When under cross-examination she vehemently denied striking Miss Soulsby.

Miss Dixon's legal counsel attempted to sway the jury by claiming that much of the evidence could be mistaken (he alleged that mistakes like this had been made in the recent past), that some was contradictory and that Mr Diery could have been mistaken about the date or the identity of the woman he had seen (even though Mr Diery had denied both these suggestions under cross-examination). He also said that if this was a capital case the jury would not convict and that Miss Dixon had lived in Rothbury for fifty years with a spotless character and reiterated that if there was any doubt the benefit should be given to Miss Dixon.

The bench retired to consider the evidence that had been put before them and upon their return the chairman (Lord Armstrong) stated that they were convinced of the guilt of Miss Dixon and that they were sentencing her to prison for a period of three months.

Just one month later a special court held at Rothbury heard a case of theft which involved juveniles, women and members of the armed services and served, at least to the magistrates, as a clear example of what could happen when impressionable young women fell foul of exploitative members of the military.

The alleged crime involved the theft of several minor household items from a caravan at Pauperhaugh on two separate occasions in April. The accused were a serving soldier, Reuben Vincent Lee, who seems to have exploited the affections of 18-year-old domestic servant Edith Caroline McKay of Brinkburn; the other accused was an unnamed 15-year-old girl. McKay was also charged with having stolen a £1 note from her mother's house at Brinkburn. Giving evidence, Miss McKay stated that on 17 April she had met Lee, whom she had known for a short time, and the two had gone for a walk along the river but had missed the bus home and that Lee had walked with her as far as Pauperhaugh where he broke into the unoccupied caravan of Mrs Gowans (who lived at Alnwick) and the two remained there until 4.00 am. When leaving, the two both stole several items including a teapot, a mirror and a piece of velvet cloth. Miss McKay said that Lee had stolen the mirror as he wanted it for shaving, while he took the cloth for polishing his boots (he also stole a cup); she took the teapot and a pair of sandshoes.

Two or three days later Miss McKay had persuaded the 15-year-old to accompany her to the caravan to get some items (mainly consisting of crockery and tableware) for her mother and said she had warned the girl not to tell her mother where they had come from. She told her mother that she had obtained the items from a fictitious Mrs Brodie. Miss McKay further admitted taking the £1 note and using it to buy a pair of shoes, stockings and a bus ticket to a dance held at Longframlington. She used the remainder to take a bus to Ashington where she stayed for the weekend, attending another dance, and spent most of Monday at Morpeth. Miss McKay declared that she had been led astray by her 'liking for the company of boys' and concluded that she 'would like to be sent to a home'.

In his evidence, Lee corroborated the story of the missed bus, adding that he and Miss McKay had remained on Pauperhaugh Bridge talking for two hours but had sought shelter from the rain in the caravan. However, he claimed that McKay had told him the caravan had not been used for two years and that her father was an officer in the RAF and the family had owned an MG car which the army had requisitioned at the start of the war. Lee admitted breaking in and taking the items, but said that it was only because he believed the woman's story and believed the caravan to be disused. He had never been in trouble before (a fact confirmed by the police), and his officer testified to his excellent character, adding that Lee was entrusted with 'hundreds of pounds of equipment, handled the rations, and was very trustworthy'.[8] The bench concluded that the ringleader of the whole affair was indeed Miss McKay and ordered that she be put on probation for two years with the condition that she spend one year at a home in Newcastle. Lee was bound over in the sum of £5 for a year, while the 15-year-old girl had her charges adjourned *sine die* (indefinitely); she was informed that the probation officer would be keeping an eye on her and that the slightest relapse into crime would see the charges reinstated immediately.

The concerns of the authorities over the possibility of declining moral standards among young people, especially women, continued throughout the war. To combat this, various local committees were set up, often with church involvement, and one of the most successful throughout north Northumberland was the Berwick Moral Welfare Committee, which went about setting up a series of lectures on moral fortitude and urged young women to take up wholesome pastimes rather than going out drinking or associating with servicemen who they did not know. In December 1943, however, the committee lost its chief worker when Miss A. Leach was ordered to rest by her doctor. A meeting held at the vicarage praised the efforts of Miss Leach who had travelled throughout the north Northumberland area in pursuance of her duties and had had significant success in reaching the young people of the area.

Two of the greatest moral concerns to the authorities in Northumberland and elsewhere were the growing numbers of children born out of wedlock and the increasing incidence of venereal disease, especially in areas hosting members of the armed forces. Although a number of propaganda campaigns were launched to try to prevent women from entering into casual liaisons (it was still usually seen as being the woman's fault), a radio broadcast on the BBC in March did raise some eyebrows. The topic was part of the *To Start You Thinking* series hosted by Dr Charles Hill and was described in the press as the 'frankest sex broadcast' in which 'nothing was barred' and as a 'free-for-all discussion – one of the frankest ever put on air by the BBC'. Taking part in the debate were Dr Hill and eight men and women aged between 16 and 19 from all over the country (including two, Robert Wheatley and Denise Ingram, from Northumberland); they were described in the press as 'sex crusaders'. The discussion was indeed, by the standards of the time, frank and covered subjects such as how youngsters were educated about sex, what could be done in the future to ensure that knowledge was gained earlier and disseminated more widely, the morality of sex before marriage, and the government's anti-VD campaigns (all of which they supported). One of the 'crusaders' said that they would be hosting a debate back home at their place of work when they returned. They described themselves as crusaders who were campaigning for sex education to be formalized in the British school system from the age of 10 upwards.

One of the Northumbrians, 18-year-old Denise Ingram, described how she had had the facts of life told to her by her mother when she 'was thirteen or fourteen [but she thought] children should be taught at a much younger age than that – ten or even younger'. Showing how the young women in particular seemed to believe that they were the issue, one commented that, before they went out with a boy, young women should know 'all about this power we have to stir him emotionally'. Dr Hill concurred and said that many girls were unaware of the power they had over men, that they 'lead them on and they are surprised at the extent to which they have led them on'.[9]

Although Northumbrian women played a highly active role in many aspects of the war effort, there were some who wished to go even further, despite official sanction. Denied the chance to play a role in the newly created LDV (Local Defence Volunteers), the women in Berwickshire were also keen to do their part in the ARP services, with a Women's Warden Corps being set up at Tweedmouth in May. A target number of fifty women was put in place and it took just a couple of days for the first thirty volunteers to enlist; the corps came under the command of Mrs R. Stirling of Union Park Road.

As previously seen, the formation of the LDV, renamed the Home Guard, had encouraged an interest in shooting in many Berwick residents and a large number of people had expressed an interest in joining the club. These included a number of women (the membership was at that point all-male) who wished to learn to accurately fire a rifle in case of invasion.[10]

People in northern Northumberland were wary of the possibility of enemy parachute landings (much of the anxiety bolstered by scare stories from France and the Low Countries). The primary role of the LDV was to report and hold out against such attacks, and commanders were aware of the vast amount of open and thinly populated countryside for which they were responsible. To help them in their efforts, it was decided to solicit the aid of those who were, for whatever reason, unable to join the LDV to volunteer as watchers. Adverts were placed in the local press calling for such volunteers and it was made clear that women would be more than welcome to serve in this non-combatant capacity.

For women the war created opportunities that would have been unthinkable in peacetime, but their role on the battlefield remained contentious throughout the war. Except in a limited few cases such as manning anti-aircraft batteries or acting as Special Operations Executive (SOE) agents in occupied Europe, women remained largely confined to non-combatant roles. Despite this, the determination of many young women to play what they saw as an active role in supporting the combat arms led to massive expansion of the Women's Auxiliary Air Force, Wrens (WRNS, Women's Royal Naval Service) and Auxiliary Territorial Service (ATS). Recruitment into the ATS was brisk in Northumberland, with many young women attracted by the wide variety of roles on offer. Trials in early 1941 had resulted in the revelation that women could serve on searchlight sites, and from July entire searchlight regiments became 'mixed' with a large number consisting of a majority of female personnel. Later in the war, women were permitted to crew mixed units of anti-aircraft batteries. Another appeal of the ATS was the fact that from July 1941 the women of the service were no longer classed as volunteers but were given full military status. Recruitment campaigns continued throughout the year with women urged to volunteer before service was made compulsory in December 1941 by the Military Service Act. Towns such as Berwick set a target of 500 volunteers for the ATS and recruitment campaigns in the local press showed the variety of roles and duties such as searchlight operator, theodolite operator, driver, mechanic, telephone operator and caterer.

A visit by the ATS's Honorary Controller-Commandant in October helped the recruitment campaign. Mary, Princess Royal and Countess of Harewood, visited an infantry training centre and opened a YWCA hut for the use of members of the ATS. After inspecting the Royal Scots and talking to several of the servicemen, the princess and her entourage moved on to inspect the cookhouse and dining hall where she talked with the cooks and praised the meat pies they were preparing for that day's lunch. The princess also visited the hospital wing where she conversed with both the staff and patients before completing her tour with an inspection of an ambulance driven by a Miss M. Swan. Moving on to her second engagement of the day, the princess was introduced to several local dignitaries. After opening and inspecting the hut, the princess declared that she was very pleased to open the hut as she was keenly aware of the facilities provided by the YWCA to women in the services. In the speeches that followed, the hut was formally named the Melbourne Hut and it was explained to the princess that the money for the hut had been sent from Australia and that the town had been selected because the head of the local ATS camp was an Australian. Speaking on behalf of the ATS, Company Sergeant Major Glass praised the hut (which was a large building) and the YWCA before thanking the princess. Keenly interested in the local ATS, the princess spoke at length to Glass and upon enquiring how long she had served in the ATS was informed that she had joined up at the very start of the war.

For a number of these young women, their patriotism resulted in their deaths. In September 1941, Aircraftwoman 1st Class Margaret Henrietta Dixon of Berwick-upon-Tweed died as a member of the WAAF; she served at RAF Elvington in Yorkshire and is buried in her home town.

Casualties among Northumbrian men were heavy and left numerous women behind to cope with bringing up a family without a main breadwinner while also coping with the grief of having lost a loved one. Many Northumbrian women also found themselves on the front lines during the war and, as we have seen, there were casualties. Among the female casualties from Northumberland were several nurses.

One of these, 32-year-old Sister Sarah Elizabeth Dixon of East Ditchburn, Eglingham, was a member of the Queen Alexandra's Imperial Nursing Service (Reserve) serving aboard the hospital ship HMHS *St David*. Although the targeting of hospital ships was a war crime and the vessel was well marked, being painted white with illuminated red crosses, the *St David* was attacked by enemy bombers off Anzio on 24 January 1944. The ship was struck by at least three bombs and sank within five minutes. The crew attempted to save the wounded and 159 people were rescued, but 22 passengers, 22 medical staff, the master and 12 crew lost their lives. Among the nursing staff lost was Sister Dixon. Elizabeth, or Bessie as she was known, had trained as a nurse at Royal Victoria Infirmary in Newcastle and had volunteered for service at the outbreak of war. Having been posted to several shore-based hospitals, she had worked on board the *St David* since May 1943. It was reported that after the bombs had hit, both Bessie and her colleague, Sister Harrison, had remained on board to aid the wounded.

Although women had banded together in the campaign for the vote, class matters separating the roles of women were still a cause for concern among many. Class issues were once again brought to the fore in January 1942 when Glendale Rural Council met at Wooler to discuss the recent appointment of

Lady Tankerville of Chillingham Castle to the bench as a Justice of the Peace. The majority of councillors, led by Councillor J. Phillips, were vehemently against the appointment, which had been made by the lord lieutenant, of yet another member of the gentry to this position. Councillor Phillips argued that the bench had 'been the preserve of the landed classes for years' and decried the fact that a tradesman or worker had no chance of being appointed. Any whose political views were not 'Tory' would also be automatically excluded (as several had been). Councillor Phillips saw the closed-shop mentality as being 'a slur and insult to the eligible women in Wooler and Glendale who could fill the post with distinction'. His pronouncements attracted agreement from a majority of the councillors present, notably T.B. Ford and G. Gallon. Phillips continued by stating that the appointment had met with a barrage of complaints locally and that it had further eroded confidence in the bench.

It seemed that during recent years a great deal of faith had been lost in the members of the bench and in their judgements and this appointment was the final straw. The matter also had a nationalistic flavour, not surprising given the state of wartime Britain because, as Councillor Phillips pointed out, Lady Tankerville was a Swede by birth and had spent a great deal of her childhood in Sweden. Indeed, he made a point of highlighting his belief that Lady Tankerville was 'a Swede by birth, by education, by upbringing and probably by tendencies'. He argued that even though she might have many fine qualities, it was solely the class she had married into that had seen her appointed, saying that 'had she married the keeper of the wild cattle at Chillingham instead of the owner she would never have been put on the bench'; a statement that once again drew praise from Councillor Ford. The clerk, Mr R. Middlemas, seems to have been more reluctant to interfere, as he stated that the appointment of JPs to the bench had 'absolutely nothing whatever to do' with the council and he baldly told the councillors: 'You, as a Council, have absolutely nothing to do with it.' Phillips and his supporters were not to be so easily put off and stated that although they realized they had nothing to do with the appointment as a body, they still had the right to lodge a complaint with the lord lieutenant. Councillor Phillips stated that the council 'ought to have' the right to appoint or nominate and advise on candidates. In the short debate that followed, one of the female councillors, Mrs Tweddell, mentioned that she knew that 'several names have been sent up from the Glendale district and they have been turned down'.[11] When the vote was taken, it was decided to put their complaints before the lord lieutenant by ten votes to two. This made no difference, however, and Lady Tankerville continued to serve.

Civil liberties had been eroded by wartime laws and by 1943 many women found themselves falling foul of the new regulations. Typical of these cases was that of canteen worker Eleanor J. Milburn of 1 Model Cottages, Rothbury, who was charged with failure to comply with a direction from the National Service Officer (it was the role of the National Service Officer to direct workers into jobs where they would be of use to the war effort). Eleanor had been ordered to take up work at a canteen in Coventry. Faced with prosecution and possible imprisonment, the accused agreed to take up the position and the case was adjourned.

A second case involved a young widow, Emma Bachinan from Longframlington, who was accused by the National Service Officer of having left employment without his permission. Mrs Bachinan and her sister had worked at a NAAFI canteen before finding similar work at an aircraft factory. After a period they requested to be allowed to work on the factory floor and were subsequently trained and employed, but Eleanor could not be employed in the department she wished to be and subsequently stated her desire to serve abroad. Due to labour shortages this request was denied, but Eleanor simply left the factory and returned home to take care of her elderly mother who was ill; she was fined £1.

These were just two cases among many similar examples. With the conversion of British society to a total war economy, it became essential to call up more workers and to have more centralized governmental power to direct workers into those areas that were deemed vital to the national war effort. The call-up of women was particularly important as they were largely an untapped source of industrial labour. By mid-January the age of women eligible for the call-up had been lowered to 19 and many young Northumbrian women found themselves directed to wartime work in munitions and aircraft factories as well as on the land in agriculture and forestry.

As well as contributing to the industry of the country, many women had of course already volunteered to serve in the women's branches of the services. One of the first WAAF non-commissioned officers to be posted for service abroad included a Belford woman whose family had a fine service record. Corporal Anne Falla was posted to the Middle East after serving for the previous two years in Britain. From Belford, Anne had previously been the manageress of Alnmouth Golf Club but after part of the course was ploughed up she decided that she would resign and serve her country by joining the WAAF. Anne had a sister who was also in the WAAF, serving in Britain, and a brother who was in the Royal Northumberland Fusiliers who had been taken prisoner in Singapore.

One of the greatest impositions placed upon women during the war was how to obtain supplies of clothing. Clothing was strictly rationed and, for many women, this presented a grave challenge in to how to present themselves. Government campaigns repeatedly urged women, and especially younger women, to make do and mend and to make their own clothing. In August 1943, young women in the Berwick area were given advice on how to create a dress said to be 'eminently suitable for the younger generation',[12] using a dark and light spotted material. Such articles were run in a regular column entitled 'Home Corner' which charged 8d for paper copies of the patterns along with 8 penny stamps.

Given the food shortages, many Northumbrian housewives looked on wartime Christmases with some concern as they were anxious to provide some semblance of the usual Christmas feast, but knew that under the circumstances it might prove difficult. Once more the local press attempted to provide some solutions and the day before Christmas Eve in 1943 the *Berwick Advertiser* included a column, under the headline 'Of Interest to Women',[13] giving guidance on preparing a Christmas or New Year meal with only limited cooking equipment or a coal fire. The suggested menu included a course of stuffed veal or other meat served with boiled root vegetables, potatoes, steamed sprouts and gravy followed by Christmas pudding with custard. The column gave a timeline of tasks to follow so that dinner would be ready by 1.00 pm.

The festive period continued to be a source of anxiety for many during the war, with shortages and separation all playing their part in causing worry to many Northumbrian women. Despite this, large numbers of women volunteered their time to ensure that those who were worse off enjoyed some semblance of a festive Christmas. In the build-up to a sixth wartime Christmas, for example, the people of the Berwick area enjoyed a large toy fair that was held at the town hall. The fair, organized by the WVS, was opened by Kathleen, Lady Armstrong, and attracted large crowds, especially of those who had young children. All proceeds went to the Red Cross with more than £400 being raised.

On 9 December 1944, the children of Holy Island were provided with a Christmas treat when the local church, along with volunteers, mainly women from the local community and from the WVS, held a tea party and present-giving. A Christmas tree was provided and a Punch and Judy show well received, although the car bringing the planned participants in the entertainment party broke down in bad weather conditions and the rest of the entertainment had to be improvised. The children were presented with more than two presents from the tree by Santa Claus (played by Police Constable Steele) and an apple each, while the under-5s also received a doll. Carol-singing was performed with gusto and concluded with the National Anthem. The next day (Sunday), a well-attended children's service was held at the Presbyterian Church and in the evening there was carol-singing in one of the islander's homes. Through such sacrifice as this, the women of Northumberland played a huge part in the county's war effort by helping to improve morale and ease tension.

The war changed forever the society in which Northumbrian women lived. Some light industry moved into the area in the aftermath of the war and women increasingly found that they had greater opportunities for employment and this in turn granted them greater autonomy and independence. For others, however, the war proved to be only a source of heartache. The decline in the traditional heavy industries of south-east Northumberland can also be traced back through the war and this decline paved the way for a recession in the area which in some parts of the county rivalled that of the 1920s and 1930s. The women of the district once again were called upon to demonstrate their fortitude and determination in the face of a government which apparently cared little for the sacrifices that had been made by the people of this isolated northern county.

Endnotes

Chapter One

1. [N]orthumberland [R]ecords [O]ffice: 851, 20. Lilburn Grange Farm, diary of an apprentice, 1842.
2. Long, Jane, *Conversations in Cold Rooms: Women, Work and Poverty in 19th Century Northumberland* (Boydell, 1999), p.93.
3. White, Walter, *Northumberland and the Border* (London, 1859).
4. Heath, Richard, *The English Peasant: Studies Historical, Local and Biographic* (London, 1893).
5. *Report of commissioners: children's, young persons' and women's employment in agriculture*, 1867.
6. Taylor, L., 'To be a Farmer's Girl: Bondagers of Border Counties', *Country Life*, October 1978, p.1110.
7. Long, *Conversations in Cold Rooms*, p.97.
8. Gubbins, Bridget, *The Curious Yards and Alleyways of Morpeth* (Greater Morpeth Development Trust, 2011), p.48.
9. Jessie Craigen was a renowned campaigner for women's suffrage, Irish Home Rule, the Co-operative Movement, and against vivisection, compulsory vaccination and the Contagious Disease Acts. Alice Cliff Scatcherd (1842–1906) was an early suffragist and a co-founder of the Women's Franchise League. Lydia Becker (1827–90) was a leader in the early suffrage movement and the founder of the *Women's Suffrage Journal*. Becker differed from many of her companions in urging the vote for unmarried women as well as claiming that there was no intellectual difference between men and women.
10. *Shields Daily Gazette*, 12 December 1893, p.4.

Chapter Two

1. *Morpeth Herald*, 9 March 1907, p.6.
2. Ibid.
3. Ibid.
4. For a detailed discussion of Emily's background and family history, see *Emily Wilding Davison: A Suffragette's Family Album* (The History Press, 2013).
5. Robert Trotter Hermon-Hodge went on to become MP for South Oxfordshire and then Croydon before becoming the 1st Baron Wyfold of Wyfold in 1919. When Jessie married, Baron Wyfold purchased a small terraced house for the couple in Newcastle.
6. It is not clear when this event took place, if indeed it did, with dates being given as 1895 and 1908 (when Emily was awarded a 1st Class (Honours) BA in Modern Languages (English and French) by the University of London).
7. Mrs Moorhouse was in fact a Maori who had been 'gifted' as a child to Mr Rhodes upon the occasion of his first marriage. When Rhodes married Sarah Ann Moorhouse following the death of his first wife, Sarah agreed to adopt Mary Anne Rhodes. Mary Anne's father had been a prominent businessman and politician and upon his death Mary Anne became the wealthiest woman in New Zealand. She married Edward Moorhouse, the younger brother of her adoptive mother, and the two moved to England. The couple had four children. Among them was William Barnard Rhodes-Moorhouse, who would have been 8 years of age at the time that Emily began working for the family. The young boy went on to posthumously be awarded the VC in 1915 while serving with the Royal Flying Corps.
8. Mrs Trevelyan was herself a half-sister of the famous Gertrude Bell.
9. Miss Garland ran for parliament unsuccessfully on no fewer than three occasions (1918, 1922 and 1929), but continued to speak for the Liberals around the country, being awarded an OBE in 1937, until her death in 1939.

10. *Morpeth Herald*, 6 February 1909, p.6.
11. *Votes for Women*, 3 September 1909, p.9.
12. *Morpeth Herald*, 4 September 1909, p.10.
13. Ibid., 11 September 1909, p.10.
14. *Morpeth Herald*, 25 September 1909, p.10.
15. The proposed budget was the first 'people's budget' intended to redistribute wealth.
16. *Morpeth Herald*, 25 September 1909, p.10.
17. Ibid., p.6.
18. Ibid., p.6.
19. *Shields Daily News*, 11 October 1909, p.3.
20. In fact, three suffragettes had already died for the cause. Mary Clark (née Pankhurst) died on Christmas Day 1910 as a result of an embolism sustained during force-feeding while in prison, and Henrietta H. Williams and Cecilia Wolseley-Haig had been killed during the brutal suppression of the riot that erupted in the wake of the deputation to the prime minister on 18 November 1910.
21. *Morpeth Herald*, 13 September 1912, p.10.
22. Ibid., 11 October 1912, p.4.
23. *Common Cause*, 24 January 1913, p.18.
24. Ibid., 28 February 1913, p.13.
25. *Common Cause*, 30 May 1913, p.14.
26. *Morpeth Herald*, 16 May 1913, p.10.
27. *Yorkshire Evening Post*, 4 July 1913, p.6.
28. Atkinson, Diane, *Rise Up Women! The Remarkable Lives of the Suffragettes* (Bloomsbury, 2019), p.412.
29. Riddell, Fern, *Death in Ten Minutes: The Forgotten Life of Radical Suffragette Kitty Marion* (Hodder & Stoughton, 2018), Kindle Edition: location 2434.
30. The owner of the scarf, Ms Barbara Goma, is clear in her view that Emily was trying to place the scarf around Anmer's neck, but her evidence is not convincing and seems to have emerged more from a determination to allege that Emily was not attempting to commit suicide.
31. Atkinson, Diane, *Rise Up, Women! The Remarkable Lives of the Suffragettes* (Bloomsbury, 2019), p.413.

32. Riddell, *Death in Ten Minutes*, Kindle Edition: location 2424.
33. Ibid.
34. *Newcastle Journal*, 14 July 1914, p.10.
35. *Common Cause*, 31 July 1914, p.18.

Chapter Three

1. *Newcastle Daily Journal*, 5 August 1914, p.7.
2. Ibid., 7 August 1914, p.6.
3. *Morpeth Herald*, 7 August 1914, p.8.
4. *Newcastle Journal*, 12 July 1915, p.7.
5. *Berwickshire News & General Advertiser*, 9 November 1915, p.3.
6. *Morpeth Herald*, 9 August 1918, p.2.
7. Ibid., 26 July 1918, p.8.
8. Ibid., 12 February 1915, p.10.
9. Ibid., 11 September 1914, p.7.

Chapter Four

1. *Alnwick & County Gazette & Guardian*, 1 September 1939, p.3.
2. Tyrer, Nicola, *They Fought in the Fields. The Women's Land Army: The Story of a Forgotten Victory* (Tempus, 2007), p.28.
3. For a fuller account of the use of female labour in Northumberland agriculture see Iredale, Dinah, *Bondagers: The History of Women Farmworkers in Northumberland and South-East Scotland* (Glendale Local History Society, 2008).
4. *Berwickshire News & General Advertiser*, 23 April 1940, p.3.
5. *Berwick Advertiser*, 10 April 1941, p.5.
6. *Alnwick & County Gazette & Guardian*, 1 September 1939, p.4.
7. *Morpeth Herald*, 11 April 1941, p.2.
8. Ibid., 23 May 1941, p.5.
9. *Daily Mirror*, 17 March 1944, p.8.
10. This was far more common than many people believe. Large numbers of women campaigned to let them join

the Home Guard as full, combat-ready members and at least one unofficial 'amazons' unit was formed. The War Office refused these demands and such units were quickly disbanded with women being largely but not wholly relegated to non-combatant duties. For more on this interesting topic see Summerfield, P. & Peniston-Bird, C., *Contesting Home Defence: Men, Women and the Home Guard in the Second World War* (Manchester University Press, 2007).

11. *Berwick Advertiser*, 15 January 1942, p.5.
12. Ibid., 5 August 1943, p.2.
13. Ibid., 23 December 1943, p.6.

Index